Life Skills English

by
Bonnie L. Walker

American Guidance Service, Inc.
Circle Pines, Minnesota 55014-1796
800-328-2560

About the Author

Bonnie L. Walker taught for sixteen years in secondary schools and college. She holds a Ph.D. in curriculum theory and instructional design from the University of Maryland, an M.Ed. in secondary education, and a B.A. in English. She studied psycholinguistics at the University of Illinois Graduate School, and was a curriculum developer at the Model Secondary School for the Deaf at Gallaudet University. She is the author of *Basic English Grammar, Basic English Composition,* and numerous workbooks, learning packages, and sound filmstrips in written expression, grammar, and usage. She was a member of Project EduTech, which investigated promising technologies to improve the delivery of special education services. Dr. Walker has written several papers on the applications of personal computers, video technology, and cable television in education. She has been the director for research and development projects funded by the U.S. Department of Education, the U.S. Department of Agriculture, and the Administration on Youth, Children, and Families. Since 1986, Dr. Walker has been president of a research and development company specializing in development of training and educational materials for special populations.

Photo Credits: p. vi—Richard Nowitz/FPG International; pp. 24, 56, 124, 178, 209, 218—Butch Housman; p. 50—Mark Lewis/Tony Stone Images; pp. 100, 223, 246—Jim and Mary Whitmer; p. 128—Farrell Grehan/FPG International; p. 130—Jon Ortner/Tony Stone Images; p. 148—David Young-Wolff/PhotoEdit; p. 156—Kevin Horan/Tony Stone Images; pp. 161, 162—Superstock; p. 172—Michelle Bridwell/PhotoEdit; p. 230—Don Smetzer/Tony Stone Images

Printed in the United States of America

ISBN 0-7854-0509-7-H (hardcover)

ISBN 0-7854-0510-0-S (softcover)

Product Number 90060 (hardcover)

Product Number 90061 (softcover)

A 0 9 8 7 6 5 4 3

2. When two words begin with the same letter, alphabetize by the second letter.

EXAMPLE	Marie	Milton
	Melvin	Monroe

Activity B   Write each list in alphabetical order on your paper.

1) prune	**2)** beef	**3)** fur
plum	biscuit	fruit
pomegranate	brown	fox
pineapple	blueberry	flame
peach	bacon	farmer

3. When the first two letters of words are the same, alphabetize by the third letter.

EXAMPLE	cab	cash
	car	cat

When the first three or more letters of words are the same, go to the next letter.

EXAMPLE	beard	beast

Activity C   Write these words in alphabetical order on your paper.

kangaroo	necklace	stuff	sixty	shirt
ship	keeper	known	stump	knight
weak	shore	sixteen	neat	stuck
knife	weather	size	show	week

4. When all the letters of a word are the same as the beginning letters of a longer word, the shorter word comes first.

EXAMPLE	am	amaze

If one of the words has an apostrophe, ignore the apostrophe.

EXAMPLE	your	you're

Activity D Write each list in alphabetical order on your paper.

1) you're	**2)** they're	**3)** any
your	their	an
you	these	animal
young	they	ant
yo-yo	the	annual

Activity E Use all of the rules that you have learned. Write each of these lists in alphabetical order on your paper.

1) thirty	**2)** record	**3)** haven
thirteen	receive	haven't
third	root	heaven
thirsty	robber	heavenly
thread	rob	heart

4) bookmobile	**5)** itch	**6)** thought
book	its	thorough
bond	item	though
bone	it	thoughtful
bookmark	Italy	thoughtless

Contents

Chapter 1

What's There and How to Find It

We are living in the "Age of Information." Television news shows and on-line computer services give us up-to-date information instantly. News shows, however, focus on current events, and not everyone has a computer available.

Where, then, can you look to find the information you need? A variety of print resources puts all kinds of information at your fingertips. Print resources include books, newspapers, magazines, catalogues, brochures, pamphlets, and even bulletin board displays.

In this book, you will learn what kinds of print resources are available to you and where to find them. You will learn the kinds of information each resource contains and how that information is arranged. Then you will be able to find the information you need quickly.

Chapter 1 provides general guidelines for finding information in print.

Goals for Learning

▶ To understand and use alphabetical order

▶ To use guide words, headings, and book divisions to find information quickly

▶ To identify key words

▶ To learn how to find information on a specific topic by using related words and topics

▶ To use the parts of a book to find information

1

Alphabetical order

The order of letters of the alphabet.

Words in **alphabetical order** are arranged according to the letters in the alphabet. Information in telephone books, indexes, and office files is arranged in alphabetical order. Knowing how to use alphabetical order can help you find information in these resources quickly.

1. Arrange words in order according to the first letter of the word.

EXAMPLE | ant   elephant

chicken   kangaroo

Activity A   Write each list in alphabetical order on your paper.

1) theater

concert

opera

movie

sports

2) robin

cardinal

starling

blue jay

wren

3) Marie

Nancy

Charles

Rosa

Doris

4) computer

monitor

printer

joystick

software

5) sofa

chair

table

lamp

piano

6) baseball

golf

tennis

hockey

football

Part A Write each list in alphabetical order on your paper.

1)	2)	3)
tank	diamond	sweet
stage	desert	sweat
sold	difference	swam
possible	dessert	swallow
taste	direction	sweep
hall	drive	swift
fog	doctor	switch
garage	door	swimming
forty	do	swim
quite	doesn't	swing
jelly	dive	swish
plate	divide	switching
foggy	dime	swept
nail	dine	sword
beyond	dirt	swung

Part B Follow the directions below. Write all your answers on your paper. Use a dictionary to check your spelling.

1) Make a list of at least ten sports.

2) List ten of the United States.

3) List the first names of ten people you know.

4) List ten kinds of animals.

5) Now go back and rewrite each of your lists in alphabetical order.

Guide words

Words at the top of a page of information given in alphabetical order. All words that come in alphabetical order between the two guide words can be found on that page.

Guide words help you find information given in alphabetical order. You will find guide words at the top of the page in many reference books. Use the guide words to help you find the page with the information you need. The first guide word is the first word on the page. The second guide word is the last word on the page. The other words on the page come in alphabetical order between these words.

Some books that have guide words are:

telephone books	atlases
dictionaries	encyclopedias

EXAMPLE

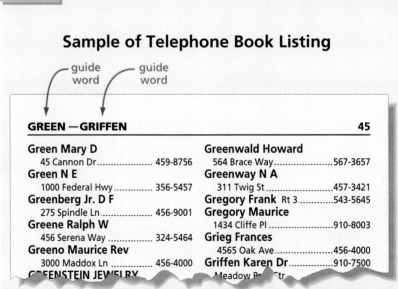

Sample of Telephone Book Listing

guide word — guide word

GREEN — GRIFFEN 45

Green Mary D
  45 Cannon Dr.................... 459-8756
Green N E
  1000 Federal Hwy.............. 356-5457
Greenberg Jr. D F
  275 Spindle Ln.................. 456-9001
Greene Ralph W
  456 Serena Way 324-5464
Greeno Maurice Rev
  3000 Maddox Ln 456-4000
GREENSTEIN JEWELRY

Greenwald Howard
  564 Brace Way......................567-3657
Greenway N A
  311 Twig St........................457-3421
Gregory Frank Rt 3.............543-5645
Gregory Maurice
  1434 Cliffe Pl 910-8003
Grieg Frances
  4565 Oak Ave......................456-4000
Griffen Karen Dr...............910-7500
  Meadow P... Ctr

Activity A   Each set of guide words below is followed by three words. Write on your paper the letters of the words that would appear on the page with each set of guide words.

Example   Guide Words: address—April

   a) add   **b)** American   **c)** appear

   Answer: b, c

1) mad—map
   a) main   **b)** maze   **c)** manage

2) sad—scream
   a) safe   **b)** sand   **c)** scratch

3) raise—remember
   a) rapidly   **b)** remain   **c)** reason

4) want ad—warp
   a) wander   **b)** wart   **c)** ward

5) fellow—fur
   a) frame   **b)** Friday   **c)** February

6) early—else
   a) east   **b)** each   **c)** elves

Activity B   Which of the names listed below would appear between the guide words shown? Write your answers on your paper.

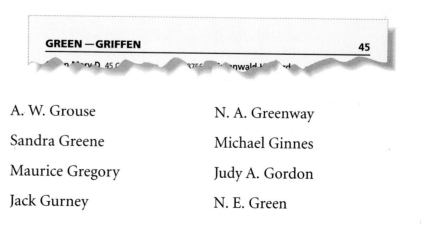

GREEN — GRIFFEN   **45**

A. W. Grouse   N. A. Greenway

Sandra Greene   Michael Ginnes

Maurice Gregory   Judy A. Gordon

Jack Gurney   N. E. Green

Sometimes you will see guide letters instead of guide words.

EXAMPLE

Sample Page from the Index of an Almanac

33 Ka - Le	
Kansas	**Key, Francis Scott** 457
(See States, U.S.)	**Kilowatt hour** 690
Agriculture 356	**Knoxville, TN** 402
Area 356, 567	**Koran** 79
Lakes, rivers 456	**Kuwait**
Population 563	Ambassadors 305
Wichita 400–401	Petroleum production .. 280
Kansas City, MO 302	— L —
Kennedy, John F. 57–58, 457	**Labor Day** 45
Kentucky	**Leap years** 102
(See States, U.S.)	**Lee, Robert E.** 458

Activity C   Use the sample page above to answer the following questions. Write your answers on your paper.

1) What pages have information about John F. Kennedy?

2) What page has information about Labor Day?

3) What pages have information about Kuwait?

4) What information about Kuwait will you find?

5) What page has information about the population of Kansas?

6) What other topic would you look up to find information about Kansas and Kentucky?

7) Would you find information about Louisiana on this page?

8) What cities in the United States can you look up from this page?

Guide Words and Headings

Some reference books have headings instead of guide words. The heading names the topic on that page.

EXAMPLE

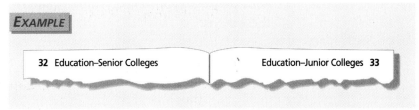

32 Education–Senior Colleges   Education–Junior Colleges 33

Guide letters and a heading may appear on the same page.

EXAMPLE

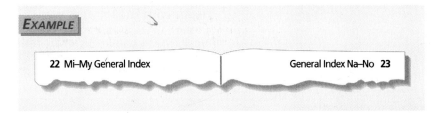

22 Mi–My General Index   General Index Na–No 23

Guide words may be placed close together on one side of the page. In the following example, the first entry on the page is "Connecticut." The last entry is "Connecticut River."

EXAMPLE

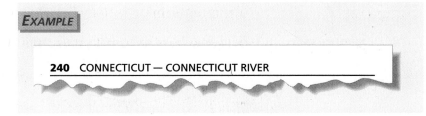

240   CONNECTICUT — CONNECTICUT RIVER

Activity D   Study the four examples below. Write answers on your paper for each of the questions that follow the examples.

a) 123   COLUMBIA RIVER—COLUMBUS
b) 22   Mi—My   General Index
c) 42   Auto Racing
d) 66   La—Ly

1) Which example shows only a heading?

2) Which example shows guide words?

3) Which example shows only guide letters?

4) Which example shows guide letters and a heading?

A Quick Way to Find the Word You Want: Dividing by Half

Here is a quick way to find words in a dictionary. First, divide your dictionary into four approximately equal parts. Follow these steps.

Step 1 Divide your dictionary in half. Open it to the middle page. You will probably find that the words begin with the letter *M*.

Step 2 Now divide the first half by half. Find the middle of the first half. You will probably find that the words begin with the letter *F*.

Step 3 Now divide the last half by half. Find the middle of the last half. You will probably find that the words begin with the letter *S*.

Then, before you look up a word, decide which part of the dictionary your word is probably in.

First Half		Last Half	
1st Quarter	2nd Quarter	3rd Quarter	4th Quarter
A B C D E F	G H I J K L M	N O P Q R S	T U V W X Y Z

Activity E In which quarter of the dictionary would you look to find each of the words below? Write each word on your paper. Beside it, write *1st, 2nd, 3rd,* or *4th.* Use a dictionary to check your answers.

1) cheese

2) neighborhood

3) toothpaste

4) animal

5) jelly

6) Thursday

7) potato

8) birthday

9) garden

10) vacation

Activity F Follow the directions below. Write your answers on your paper.

- Find the following words in any dictionary.
- Use the "divide by half" method.
- Write down the time you begin.
- Write down the guide words from each page.
- Write down the time you finish.
- Try to do this in less than five minutes.

1) wisdom   **6)** recognize

2) pleasant   **7)** garage

3) fierce   **8)** flashlight

4) chipmunk   **9)** machine

5) canoe   **10)** blueberry

Activity G Follow the directions below.

- Write the list of words below in alphabetical order on your paper.
- Find the words in a dictionary.
- Use the guide words to help.
- Use the "divide by half" method.
- Time yourself.
- Try to beat five minutes.

1) usually   **6)** meadow

2) perhaps   **7)** harness

3) gnaw   **8)** recognize

4) island   **9)** butcher

5) astonish   **10)** delicious

Part A   Each set of guide words or letters is followed by four words. Write on your paper the letters of the words that would appear on the page with each set of guide words.

1) adventure—belt
   a) among   b) brick   c) address   d) arrange

2) damp—doesn't
   a) danger   b) die   c) dirt   d) don't

3) spider—study
   a) sparkle   b) steer   c) straw   d) stump

4) weather—worry
   a) weak   b) welcome   c) we're   d) worse

5) purple—softly
   a) puzzle   b) prove   c) softness   d) soft

6) va—ye
   a) yellow   b) village   c) you'll   d) year

7) Jackson—Johnson
   a) Jason   b) Jones   c) Jordon   d) Johns

8) Al—Fl
   a) Alaska   b) Alabama   c) Hawaii   d) Arizona

9) Ad—Ar
   a) Adams   b) Aiken   c) Alcott   d) Anders

Part B   Use the "divide by half" method to find these words in a dictionary. Write on your paper the guide words from each page.

1) wrap
2) scatter
3) seventy
4) jewel
5) eagle

6) airport
7) passenger
8) holiday
9) Friday
10) quilt

When you don't know the answer to a question, you can often find the answer by looking it up. First, however, you must know what to look up. A **subject** or **topic** is whatever you want to know about. A **subtopic** is a topic that is part of another topic.

Topic (subject)

What you want to find out about.

The word you look up to find information to answer a question is called a **key word**. A key word can be a topic, a subtopic, or another word related to the question. In the following example, *spider* and *poisonous spider* are key words. Those are the words you might look up to find the answer to the question.

Subtopic

A topic that is part of a larger topic.

Key word

A word that names what you want to find out about.

EXAMPLE   Question: Which spiders are poisonous to humans?

Topic: spider

Subtopic: poisonous spider

Activity A   Write each pair of key words on your paper. Beside each key word, write *topic* or *subtopic*.

Example   tool—**topic**   saw—**subtopic**

1) fruit   blueberries

2) oak tree   plants

3) mosquito   insect

4) magazine   *Time*

5) game   checkers

6) Amy Tan   writer

7) plate   dishes

8) movie   *Apollo 13*

What to Do When You Can't Find Your Topic

Use Synonyms

Even when you know what topic to look up, you may not find it listed. When that happens, try to think of another name for your topic. A word that has the same or a similar meaning as another word is a **synonym**. Try thinking of a synonym for your topic. Then look up that word.

Synonym

A word with the same or nearly the same meaning as another word.

EXAMPLES	Key Word	Synonym
	insect	bug
	nations	countries
	author	writer

Activity B   Write on your paper the letter of the word that is a synonym for the word given.

1) lady
   a) person   **b)** Whoopi Goldberg   **c)** woman

2) stairs
   a) steps   **b)** elevator   **c)** building

3) dinner
   a) meal   **b)** supper   **c)** food

4) country
   a) nation   **b)** United States   **c)** place

5) movie
   a) theater   **b)** *Star Wars*   **c)** film

Activity C   Write a synonym on your paper for each topic below. You may use a dictionary.

1) railroads   **6)** soda

2) blizzards   **7)** dinner

3) agriculture   **8)** physician

4) media center   **9)** bug

5) banquet   **10)** songs

Look for Broad and Narrow Topics

You may not find your topic listed because it is too narrow. Then you should look for a broader topic.

EXAMPLES	Narrow Topic	Broad Topic
	collies	dogs
	tornadoes	weather

Sometimes your topic may be too broad. Then you should look for a narrower topic.

EXAMPLES	Broad Topic	Narrow Topic
	ships	Constitution
	transportation	trains
	patriotic songs	"America the Beautiful"

Activity D Write another word on your paper that you might look up for each topic listed below. Use a dictionary to help identify synonyms as well as broader and narrower topics.

Examples	coffee	**beverages**
	metropolitan areas in the U.S.	**U.S. cities**
	higher education in Canada	**Canadian colleges**

USING WHAT YOU HAVE LEARNED

Suppose you want to know what a baby kangaroo is called, but you can't find the word *kangaroo* listed. What other word could you look up?

- Write one or two ideas.
- Then try looking them up.
- Share what you find with a partner.

1) Miami
2) Cars
3) Mars
4) Lawyers
5) Doctors
6) Kings
7) France
8) Football
9) Highways
10) Thanksgiving

11) Famous writers
12) Famous singers
13) Famous teachers
14) High schools
15) African history
16) Cities with harbors
17) Poodles
18) "The Star-Spangled Banner"
19) Films
20) Songwriters

Use Related Words and Topics

If you can't find information on a specific topic, look for **related topics**. A related topic is one that is connected or associated with another topic.

> **EXAMPLE** If you wanted to open a pizza shop, you might not be able to find any information on pizza shops. Then you might look for information on related topics.
>
> Specific topic: Pizza Shop
>
> Related topics: Italian Cooking
>
> Running a Small Business
>
> Fast Foods

Activity E Write at least one related topic on your paper for each topic listed below. You may use a dictionary.

Example Building a fireplace
Related topics: **bricklaying, heating systems**

1) Skiing

2) Vegetable gardening

3) Raising poodles

4) Learning word processing

5) Making model cars

6) Playing the guitar

7) Video games

8) Becoming a Licensed Practical Nurse (LPN)

9) Sailboating

10) Becoming a bus driver

Part A   Write at least one key word on your paper for each question below.

Example   In what years was baseball's World Series not played?
Key words: **baseball, World Series**

1) Who won the Oscar for best actress in 1939?
2) What is the population of Akron, Ohio?
3) What team won the National Basketball Association playoffs in 1994?
4) In what state is Yellowstone National Park?
5) What is the most popular magazine in the United States?

Part B   For each question, write at least two key words and a synonym or related topic on your paper. You may use a dictionary for this activity.

Example   Who was the president of the United States during World War II?

Key words:	**World War II**
	U.S. presidents
Synonym:	**Leaders**
Related topic:	**Wars**

1) Who won the World Series in 1939?
2) What is the weather like in Minneapolis?
3) Who won the Nobel Peace Prize in 1952?
4) What were the names of Henry VIII's six wives?
5) What is the capital city of Mexico?
6) How tall is the Washington Monument?
7) How many students attend Harvard University?
8) What is the closest shoe store?
9) How many strings does a guitar have?
10) Did any volcanoes erupt last year?
11) Which restaurants serve Chinese food?

Chapter

A part of a book.

Index

An alphabetical list of main topics covered in a book.

Preface

An introduction to a book.

Reference book

A book that contains facts about a specific topic or on several topics.

Table of contents

A list of the chapters or sections of a book and the page numbers on which the chapters or sections begin.

When you look up information, you usually look in some type of **reference book**. A reference book is a book of facts. A reference book may contain facts on a single topic or on several topics.

You can usually tell whether a book has the information you need by looking at the book's **table of contents** and its **index**. A table of contents is a list of chapter titles at the beginning of a book. An index is a list of topics in a book, arranged in alphabetical order. An index is usually found at the back of a book.

The Table of Contents

The table of contents is in the front of a book. When you look at the table of contents, you can see at a glance what information the book contains and how it is divided. Some books contain a **preface**, which is an introduction to a book. Many books are divided into **chapters**. A chapter is part or section of a book. In a table of contents, the chapter titles are listed in the order that they appear in the book. The page numbers on which the chapters begin are also listed.

EXAMPLES

Sea Shells **Contents**

Preface
1. Types of mollusks 3
2. Collecting marine shells 11
3. Locations 18
    California 19
    Carolinas 20
    Hawaiian Islands 22

Car Care *Contents*

1. Buying a car 2
2. Car insurance 17
3. Financing 34
4. Cooling system 56
5. Engine oil 64
6. Tires 73
7. Emergencies 91
    Index 121

Activity A Use the sample tables of contents above to answer the questions below and at the top of the next page. Write your answers on your paper.

1) Is there a chapter in *Car Care* about brakes?

2) You want to collect sea shells in Hawaii. Will the book *Sea Shells* help?

3) On what page does the chapter about tires begin? On what page does that chapter end?

4) Which book has an index?

5) Which book has a preface?

6) Will *Car Care* give you information about buying car insurance?

7) How many chapters does *Car Care* have?

An Index

Almost all reference books and many nonfiction books have an index at the back. An index lists the main topics covered in the book in alphabetical order. Subtopics appear under some of the main topics. The subtopics are also listed in alphabetical order. Page numbers are listed beside each topic and subtopic.

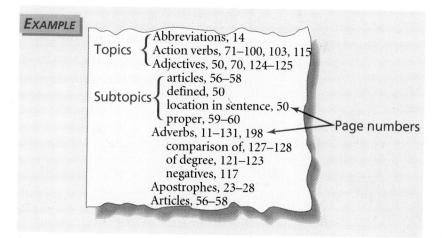

EXAMPLE

Topics {
Abbreviations, 14
Action verbs, 71–100, 103, 115
Adjectives, 50, 70, 124–125

Subtopics {
articles, 56–58
defined, 50
location in sentence, 50
proper, 59–60
Adverbs, 11–131, 198 — Page numbers
comparison of, 127–128
of degree, 121–123
negatives, 117
Apostrophes, 23–28
Articles, 56–58

Activity B   Use the sample index above to answer these questions. Write the answers on your paper.

1) Will page 77 tell you about action verbs?

2) Can you find facts about action verbs on page 112?

3) Which pages tell you about apostrophes?

4) Which page has a definition of an adjective?

5) Which pages tell you about articles?

6) To what other topic is "articles" related?

7) Name one subtopic under the main topic "Adverbs."

8) Which pages tell you about adverbs of degree?

9) How many pages tell you about proper adjectives?

10) How many pages tell you about abbreviations?

More About Indexes

To refer means to direct someone for information.

> **EXAMPLE**   Refer to page 87 for more information on computers.

Many indexes list **cross references**. A cross reference is a related topic that you can refer to. Some cross references tell you where to look to find the information you need. Other cross references tell you where to look to find more information on your topic.

> **EXAMPLE**
>
> Orlando, Fla, 641
>   Mayor, 56
>   Population, 87
>   (see also States of the U.S.)   ←— Cross reference
> Oscars (see Academy Awards)
>   **P**
> Pacific Ocean
>   Area, depth, 354
>   Discovery, 355

Activity C   Use the sample index above to answer these questions. Write your answers on your paper.

1) Name three pages with facts about Orlando, Florida.

2) What other subject can you look up to find facts about Orlando, Florida?

3) What topic must you look up to find out who has won an Oscar?

4) Look carefully at the example above. There are two kinds of cross references. What is the difference between "see also" and "see"?

Activity D   Use the table of contents and index of this textbook to write the answers to the following questions.

1) Does this book have a chapter about using a dictionary?

2) Which pages tell you about using an encyclopedia?

3) Which chapter tells you how to use the Yellow Pages?

4) Which page has a sample business letter?

Lesson Review   Study the sample table of contents and index from the two different books. Write the answers to these questions on your paper.

From *Book of Maps*:

Contents

From *Things to Make*:

Index

Book of Maps

1) On what page is there a map of South America?

2) Does the book have a map that shows only Texas?

3) Is there a map that shows only Alaska?

4) Does this book have a preface?

Things to Make

5) What page tells you how to find material?

6) Which pages tell you about using match boxes?

7) You can find out about pot holders on page 80. What other page will help?

Part A Rewrite the following list of words in alphabetical order on your paper.

you've	you	shade	brook
seventy	brooks	seven	wrote
forest	forget	act	action
English	elves	forgot	elf
you're	lose	write	puzzle
loose	mind	we're	mine

Part B Three words follow each set of guide words or guide letters. Write the letters of the words that would appear on the page with each set of guide words or guide letters.

1) Grouse—Gurney
   a) Green   b) Gordon   c) Guiness

2) mi—mu
   a) monsters   b) music   c) meadows

3) package—pickles
   a) pack   b) passenger   c) pillows

4) sh—sw
   a) shadow   b) sleigh   c) soap

5) Alaska—Colorado
   a) Alabama   b) Alaska   c) Connecticut

Part C For each question, write at least two key words and a synonym or related topic on your paper. You may use a dictionary for this activity.

1) How many people live in Tucson, Arizona?

2) Which baseball team won the World Series six years in a row?

3) What was the top film of 1994?

4) What is the average amount of rain each year in Arizona?

5) Where is the Amazon rain forest?

Part D   Write the answers to these questions on your paper.

1) Which book part lists topics in alphabetical order—a table of contents or an index?

2) Where in a book do you usually find the index?

3) Where would you look to find the table of contents?

4) Where would you find the preface?

5) If you looked up *skeleton* in the index of your science textbook and saw the following, what would you learn?

Skeleton   (see Human Body)

Part E   Use the table of contents and the index of this book to answer the following questions. Write your answers on your paper.

1) Which chapter tells you about using a library?

2) Which page tells about the chamber of commerce?

3) On which page do you find out how to place a classified ad?

4) How many pages does Chapter 6 have?

5) Which chapter and lesson tells you about cable TV?

6) Can you get help from this book about giving a speech?

7) What is the first page of the chapter about newspapers, television, and radio? What is the last page?

8) On what page does the index begin?

9) Does this book have a preface?

10) Which pages tell you about job application forms?

Test Taking Tip   Before you begin an exam, skim through the whole test to find out what is expected of you.

Chapter 2

Answering Questions About Words

Dictionaries come in all sizes. There are very large dictionaries with hundreds of thousands of words. There are smaller dictionaries that include only the most commonly used words. Every dictionary, however, contains words and information about those words.

No dictionary is ever totally complete. New words and meanings are always being added. Most of the dictionaries that are used in classrooms and homes are abridged, or shortened. This means that some words have been left out of these dictionaries. Unabridged, or complete, dictionaries have not been shortened. They are large books, often in several volumes. Libraries usually have unabridged dictionaries.

In Chapter 2, you will learn about different features of dictionaries and how to use the features.

Goals for Learning

▶ To understand how a dictionary is organized

▶ To identify the different parts of a dictionary entry

▶ To use a dictionary to find word meanings

▶ To use a dictionary to check spelling

▶ To use a dictionary as a reference book

Dictionary

A book that contains an alphabetical listing of words and their meanings.

A **dictionary** is a book that lists words and some facts about the words. Every dictionary has **entries**, guide words, and **keys**. An entry is a word that is described in a dictionary. All entries are listed in bold type and in alphabetical order. A key is an explanation of symbols and abbreviations used in each entry. Here is a sample dictionary page.

Entry

A listing in a dictionary. An entry provides facts about a word.

Key

A guide to the symbols and abbreviations used in each entry.

guide words

entries listed in alphabetical order

| mouth | 314 | myth |

mouth (mouth), *n., pl.,* **mouths** (mou<u>th</u>z). **1.** an opening through which a man or animal takes in food. **2.** a part of a river where its water empties into a larger body: *the mouth of the Nile.* [German *mund*] **mouth´less,** *adj.*

mov•ie (mōō´vē), *n.* **1.** See **motion picture. 2.** a motion-picture theater: *The movie is next to the drugstore.* **3. movies,** motion pictures: *The people go to the movies.* [MOV(ING PICTURE) + -IE]

Mu•si•al (myōō´ zē əl) *n.* Stanley Frank ("Stan the Man") Born 1920, U.S. baseball player.

mu•sic (myōō´ zik), *n.* **1.** a sound which expresses ideas and feelings using rhythm, melody, and harmony. **2.** a musical work for singing or playing. [Greek *mousikē* (the art) of the Muse]

mu•si•cal (myōō´ zi kəl), *adj.* **1.** of, related to, or making music: a musical instrument. **2.** liking or skilled at music: a musical person. —*n.* **3.** See **musical comedy.** [Latin *mūsicāl(is)*] **mu´si•cal•ly,** *adv.* —**mū´si•cal•ness,** *n.*

mu´sical com´edy, a play with music, including singing and dancing.

myth (mith) *n.* a traditional or legendary story.

---

a - act, ā - āble, â - dâre, ä - ärm, e - ebb, ē - ēven, i - it, ī - īce,
o - hot, ō - ōver, ô - ôrder, oi - oil, ŏŏ - bŏŏk, ōō - lōōt, ou - out,
u - up, û - ûrge, ch - chief, ng - sing, sh - shoe, th - thin, <u>th</u> - <u>th</u>is,
zh - vision,   ə = *a* as in *ago*.

pronunciation key

Activity A   Use the sample dictionary page above. Write on your paper the word that completes each sentence below and on page 27.

1) The guide words are at the _____ of the page.

2) The first entry on page 314 is _____.

---

3) The last entry on the page is _____.

4) The pronunciation key is at the _____ of the page.

5) There are _____ entries on page 314.

Most dictionary entries contain the same basic features. The entries below provide examples of these features.

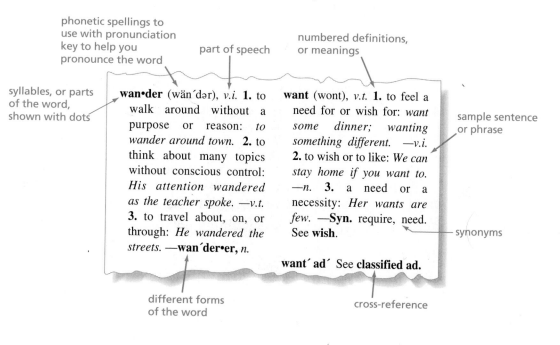

phonetic spellings to use with pronunciation key to help you pronounce the word

part of speech

numbered definitions, or meanings

syllables, or parts of the word, shown with dots

wan•der (wän´dər), *v.i.* **1.** to walk around without a purpose or reason: *to wander around town.* **2.** to think about many topics without conscious control: *His attention wandered as the teacher spoke.* —*v.t.* **3.** to travel about, on, or through: *He wandered the streets.* —**wan´der•er,** *n.*

want (wont), *v.t.* **1.** to feel a need for or wish for: *want some dinner; wanting something different.* —*v.i.* **2.** to wish or to like: *We can stay home if you want to.* —*n.* **3.** a need or a necessity: *Her wants are few.* —**Syn.** require, need. See **wish.**

want´ ad´ See **classified ad.**

sample sentence or phrase

synonyms

different forms of the word

cross-reference

Activity B Use the sample entries and pronunciation key to answer the questions. Write your answers on your paper.

1) How many meanings are given for *wander?*

2) What are two synonyms for *want?*

3) What is another form of the verb *wander?*

4) Does the *a* in *wander* have the same sound as the *a* in *want?*

5) Which two entries have cross-references?

Pronouncing a Word

You may look up a word in a dictionary to find out how it is pronounced. A dictionary entry has three features that can help you pronounce a word.

Syllable

A part of a word with one vowel sound.

1. The word is divided into **syllables** that are separated by dots. A syllable is a part of a word or a unit of speech that has one vowel sound.

Accent mark

A mark that shows which part of a word to stress when pronouncing the word.

2. One of the syllables has an **accent mark** (´). This mark shows which syllable to **stress** when you pronounce the word. When you stress a syllable, you emphasize that syllable more than the other syllables in the word.

Stress

To pronounce a syllable with more emphasis than the other syllables in the word.

3. Each entry gives the phonetic spelling for the word. The pronunciation key can help you understand the phonetic spelling. The key is usually at the bottom of the page. The pronunciation key lists words that you probably know how to say. Match the vowel sound in the word in the pronunciation key with the vowel sound in the entry word. That way you can figure out how to say the word.

EXAMPLE

mu•si•cal (myoo′zi kəl)

a - act, ā - āble, â - dâre, ä - ärm, e - ebb, ē - ēven, i - it, ī - īce,
o - hot, ō - ōver, ô - ôrder, oi - oil, oo - book, oo - loot, ou - out,
u - up, û - ûrge, ch - chief, ng - sing, sh - shoe, th - thin, th - this,
zh - vision, ə = a as in *ago*.

The phonetic spelling of *musical* shows that the vowel sound in the third syllable is the same as the *a* sound in *ago*. This vowel sound is called a schwa. It is shown with the symbol ə. You often hear the schwa vowel sound in unstressed syllables.

Activity C Look at the sample dictionary entry and the pronunciation key below. Write your answers to the questions that follow.

as•sem•bly (ə sem´ blē)

a - act, ā - āble, â - dâre, ä - ärm, e - ebb, ē - ēven, i - it, ī - īce,
o - hot, ō - ōver, ô - ôrder, oi - oil, o͞o - bo͝ok, o͞o - lo͞ot, ou - out,
u - up, û - ûrge, ch - chief, ng - sing, sh - shoe, th - thin, th - this,
zh - vision,   ə = a as in ago.

1) How many syllables does *assembly* have? How do you know?
2) Which syllable should you stress when pronouncing *assembly*?
3) How can you tell which syllable to stress?
4) What sound does the vowel in the first syllable have?
5) What sound does the vowel in the last syllable have?

Abbreviation

A shortened form of a written word.

Abbreviations

Some of the features of a dictionary entry are abbreviated. An **abbreviation** is a shortened form of a written word.

You can learn what some common abbreviations stand for in a dictionary entry. Knowing these abbreviations can help you understand the use and meaning of the word you are looking up.

You can see common abbreviations in this dictionary entry.

EXAMPLE

noun (*n.*)   plural (*pl.*)

mouth (mouth), *n., pl.,* **mouths** (mouthz).   **1.** an opening through which a man or animal takes in food.   **2.** a part of a river where its water empties into a larger body: *the mouth of the Nile.* [German *mund*] **mouth´less,** *adj.*

adjective (*adj.*)

Parts of Speech

In a dictionary entry, abbreviations for parts of speech usually follow the phonetic spelling of the word. This abbreviation tells you what part of speech the word is. Abbreviations for parts of speech may also appear in other parts of the entry if the word can be more than one part of speech.

Here is a list of abbreviations for parts of speech and their meanings.

n.	=	noun: names a person, place, thing, or idea.
pron.	=	pronoun: replaces a noun (he, she, me, that, everyone).
adj.	=	adjective: describes a noun or pronoun.
v.	=	verb: expresses action or a state of being (run, sing, look, become).
adv.	=	adverb: tells how, when, where, or how much (very, slowly, quickly).
prep.	=	preposition: shows a relationship between a noun or pronoun and another part of the sentence (in, above, near).
conj.	=	conjunction: connects sentences or parts of a sentence (and, because, or).
interj.	=	interjection: a word that expresses feelings (Oh! Wow!)

In most dictionary entries, a verb is labeled *v.t.* or *v.i.* rather than just *v.* Some verbs can be both transitive and intransitive.

v.t.	=	verb, transitive: a verb that needs an object to complete its meaning. An object is a noun or a pronoun.
v.i.	=	verb, intransitive: a verb that does not have an object.

EXAMPLE	Transitive verb:	He **throws** the ball. (*Ball* is the direct object.)
	Intransitive:	He **throws** hard. (*Hard* is an adverb.)

Singular and Plural

Most words become plural by adding -*s*. If the word you look up forms its plural in a different way, you may see the abbreviation *pl.* followed by the word in its plural form.

> **sing.** = singular: one person, place, thing, or idea.
> **pl.** = plural: more than one person, place, thing, or idea.

en•try (en´trē), *n.*, *pl.*, **entries.** **1.** the act of entering: *The army made its entry into the city.* **2.** a statement or item entered in a book. [From Latin *intrāre*, to enter.]

Synonyms

Another abbreviation you might see in a dictionary entry is *Syn.* This stands for the word *synonym.* Synonyms are words with similar meanings. In a dictionary entry, the words that follow the abbreviation *Syn.* are synonyms for the word you looked up.

> **Syn.** = synonym: a word with the same or nearly the same meaning as another word.

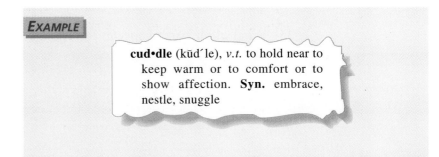

cud•dle (kūd´le), *v.t.* to hold near to keep warm or to comfort or to show affection. **Syn.** embrace, nestle, snuggle

Activity D   Use these sample dictionary entries to answer the questions below. Write your answers on your paper.

> **i•vo•ry** (ī′ və rē, ī′ vrē), *n., pl.* **-ies** [ME < OF *ivurie*]   **1.** the hard creamy-white dentine that composes the tusks of the elephant, walrus, etc.   **2.** this substance used to make carvings, billiard balls, etc.   **3.** a yellowish-white color.   **4.** something made of ivory (as dice or piano keys) or of a similar substance. –**ivory** *adj.*

> **change** (chānj), *v.t.*   **1.** to cause to be different in some way.   **2.** to replace with something else.   *v.i.* **1.** to become different in some way.   **2.** to go from one stage to another. **Syn.** alter, vary, shift   –*n.* **1.** a shift from one thing to another.

1) What abbreviations appear in the two entries? Write the abbreviations and their meanings in order.

2) What two parts of speech can *ivory* be?

3) What is the plural spelling of *ivory*?

4) Is *change* a transitive or intransitive verb? How do you know?

5) What are three synonyms for *change?*

6) What other part of speech can *change* be?

Part A Number your paper from 1 to 8. Write the letter of the correct matching definition beside the number of the term.

Example **1)** c

1) dictionary

2) entry words

3) guide words

4) pronunciation key

5) abbreviation

6) synonym

7) cross-reference

8) plural

a) A related entry

b) More than one

c) A book that lists words

d) Explanation of symbols used in phonetic spelling

e) Words listed in a dictionary

f) Words at the top of a dictionary page showing the first and last entries on that page

g) A word that has almost the same meaning as another word

h) A shortened form of a written word

Part B Write on your paper the full word or words for each abbreviation.

1) pl.

2) n.

3) syn.

4) adj.

5) prep.

6) v.i.

7) v.t.

8) adv.

9) conj.

10) pron.

Part C Write the answers to these questions on your paper.

1) Where are the guide words in a dictionary?

2) How are syllables separated in a dictionary entry?

3) What does an accent mark tell you?

4) Where is the pronunciation key usually found?

Word Meanings

You may look up a word in a dictionary to find out what the word means. A dictionary entry gives one or more meanings for each word listed. Each meaning is numbered. Sample phrases or sentences are often given for each meaning. If a word can be more than one part of speech, different meanings for each part of speech are also given.

EXAMPLE

> **o•ver•cast** (ō′və r kast), *n.* **1.** a covering, esp. of clouds.   **2.** an arch in a mine, supporting an overhead passage.   *−adj.* **3.** cloudy; dark; said of the sky or weather.   **4.** Sewing made with overcasting.   *−v.t.* **-cast′, -cast′ing, 5.** to overcloud; darken. **6.** *Sewing* to sew over an edge of material with long, loose stitches so as to prevent raveling.

If you know how a word is used in a sentence, you can figure out which meaning applies. In the following examples, the word *overcast* is used three different ways. The number in parentheses after each sentence matches the number of the meaning in the dictionary entry above.

EXAMPLE

Because the sky was **overcast**, she grabbed her umbrella. (3)

Our sewing teacher showed us how to **overcast** the edges of the material. (6)

The miners knew the **overcast** would give way in an earthquake. (2)

Activity A   Number your paper from 1 to 5. Beside each number write the part of speech and meaning of *overcast* as it is used in the sentence. Copy the meanings from the dictionary entry on page 34.

Example   Today will be overcast. (Adjective, cloudy, dark; said of the sky or weather.)

1) The overcast fell down and trapped the miners.
2) Mrs. Gomez overcast the seams in Marie's shirt.
3) The overcast hem would not ravel easily.
4) An overcast sky was expected on Monday.
5) The overcast made everyone feel gloomy.

When you look up a word to find its meaning, the meaning may contain other words that you do not know. When that happens, you will have to look up the unfamiliar words. This can take several steps.

Here is an example of what might happen when you want to find out a word's meaning.

EXAMPLE   You are reading an article about your favorite baseball team in the sports section of the newspaper. You come to this sentence:

"The Cubs will play a twin bill Sunday afternoon against the Mets."

You think you know what *twin bill* means, but you decide to check its meaning in the dictionary. When you look up *twin bill,* what you find is below.

> **twin bill** *n.* same as   **1.** DOUBLE FEATURE.
> **2.** DOUBLEHEADER (sense 2)

Words in capital letters are synonyms and cross references for the entry word. Therefore, you look up both *double feature* and *doubleheader.* When you look up *doubleheader,* what you find is below.

> **dou•ble•head•er** (dub əl hed´ər), *n.* **1.** a train pulled by two locomotives. **2.** two games played on the same day between two teams in succession.

The cross-reference for *doubleheader* tells you to look at "sense 2." When you look at meaning 2, you learn that a doubleheader means that two games are played on the same day in succession. To understand exactly what that means, you also look up *succession.*

> **suc•ces•sion** (sək sesh´ ən), *n.* the coming of one person or thing after another in order.

Finally, you know what the sentence in the article means:

On Sunday afternoon, the Cubs will play two games against the Mets. The second game will be played right after the first one.

Activity B   Use a dictionary to find the meanings of the words in bold. Look up any words that you do not know. Then rewrite each sentence on your paper. Replace the words in bold with their meanings. You may have to add some words so that the sentence makes sense.

Example   Mr. Gomez realized that his son Eddie was **precocious.**
Mr. Gomez realized that his son Eddie was extremely mature for his age.

1) The Williams family spent their summer vacation at a **resort.**
2) "I'm doing some **reconnaissance** work," said the police officer.
3) Marie does not **resemble** her twin sister Michelle in any way.
4) Chris said that O. Henry wrote under a **pseudonym.**
5) "O'er the **ramparts** we watched," is a line from the "The Star-Spangled Banner."
6) John works for Anita Valdez, a **reputable** attorney.
7) After their long **trek,** Al and Justin were **ravenous.**
8) The house was under **quarantine** because someone had **whooping cough.**
9) The coach hoped that the **rookie** would be an **asset** to the team.

Word Origins

Etymology

The study of the history of a word.

You may look up a word to learn its history, or **etymology**. Over time, a word can change its spelling, its pronunciation, and its meaning. All of these changes are part of the history of the word.

Origin

The beginning of something.

When you look up a word to learn its **origin**, you may see the symbol <. This symbol means "**derived** from," or "comes from." The information that follows the symbol < explains the word's history. Some dictionaries use the word *from* or the abbreviation *fr* instead of the symbol <. Here are some other abbreviations you may see when you look up a word's history. They stand for the languages in which the words were first used.

Derived

To come from. (Many English words are derived from other languages.)

OE = Old English	ME = Middle English	L = Latin
G = German	Gk = Greek	It = Italian
OF = Old French	F = French	S = Spanish

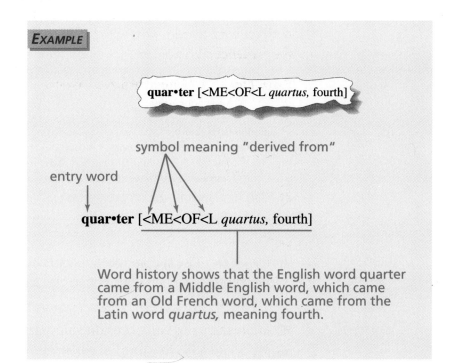

EXAMPLE

quar•ter [<ME<OF<L *quartus,* fourth]

symbol meaning "derived from"

entry word

quar•ter [<ME<OF<L *quartus,* fourth]

Word history shows that the English word quarter came from a Middle English word, which came from an Old French word, which came from the Latin word *quartus,* meaning fourth.

Activity C Find the etymology of the two entry words in the two sample entries below. Write your answers to the questions on your paper.

> **quar•ter** (kwôr´ tər), *n.* [<ME<OF<L *quartus,* fourth]
> **1.** a fourth of something. **2.** a fourth of a year. **3.** one fourth of an hour. **4.** one fourth of a dollar, 25¢.
>
> **que•ry** (kwēr´ ē), *n.* [<L *quaerere,* ask] **1.** a question, inquiry. **2.** a question mark. –*v.t.* **que´ried, que´ry•ing** to question.

1) What marks are around the etymology of a word?
2) What was the most recent origin of the word *quarter?* (The name of the language is abbreviated.)
3) In what language did the word *query* begin?
4) What does the Latin word *quartus* mean?
5) What does the Latin word *quaerere* mean?

Other Forms

A dictionary often gives other forms of the entry word followed by their parts of speech.

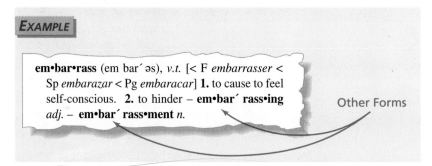

EXAMPLE

> **em•bar•rass** (em bar´ əs), *v.t.* [< F *embarrasser* < Sp *embarazar* < Pg *embaracar*] **1.** to cause to feel self-conscious. **2.** to hinder – **em•bar´ rass•ing** *adj.* – **em•bar´ rass•ment** *n.*

Other Forms

Activity D Use the sample entry to complete the following. Write your answers on your paper. Use a dictionary for help if you need it.

1) Write the word *embarrass* on your paper.
2) Write the adjective form of *embarrass.*
3) Write the noun form of *embarrass.*
4) Write a sentence for each of the two meanings of *embarrass.*

Differences in Dictionary Entries

No two dictionaries are exactly alike. An entry for the same word in different dictionaries may contain different information.

Here are examples of entries for the word *home run* from four different dictionaries. Each entry presents the definition in a slightly different way.

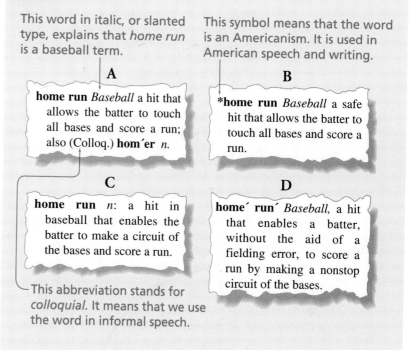

EXAMPLE

This word in italic, or slanted type, explains that *home run* is a baseball term.

This symbol means that the word is an Americanism. It is used in American speech and writing.

A

home run *Baseball* a hit that allows the batter to touch all bases and score a run; also (Colloq.) **hom´er** *n.*

B

*home run *Baseball* a safe hit that allows the batter to touch all bases and score a run.

C

home run *n*: a hit in baseball that enables the batter to make a circuit of the bases and score a run.

This abbreviation stands for *colloquial.* It means that we use the word in informal speech.

D

home´ run´ *Baseball,* a hit that enables a batter, without the aid of a fielding error, to score a run by making a nonstop circuit of the bases.

Activity E Use the sample entries to answer these questions. Write your answers on your paper.

1) Which of the entries is the simplest to understand—A, B, C, or D? Why?

2) Which entry gives extra information? What is that information?

3) What is another term for *home run?*

4) Which entries give the part of speech? What part of speech is *home run?*

Most dictionaries give the same basic information for a word. Some dictionaries give more information, and some give less. Different dictionaries may also give information in a different order.

A

hock•ey (håk´ ē) *n.* [prob.<OFr. *hoquet,* bent stick] **1.** a team game played on ice skates, with curved sticks and a rubber disk (puck). **2.** a similar game played on foot on a field with a small ball.

B

hock•ey (hok´ ē) *n.* **1.** See **ice hockey. 2.** See **field hockey.** [earlier *hockie*]

field´ hockey, a game, played on a rectangular field, having a netted goal at each end, in which two teams of 11 players each compete in driving a small leather-covered ball into the other's goal, each player being equipped with a stick having a curved end or blade that is flat on one side and rounded on the other.

Activity F   Use the information in the sample entries to answer these questions. Write your answers on your paper.

1) What is the origin of *hockey?*

2) How was *hockey* probably spelled in the past?

3) Under which letter—A or B—are cross-references given? Which entry word has the cross-references and what are they?

4) What is the difference between the playing surfaces in the two kinds of hockey?

A dictionary entry may include symbols and abbreviations that have not been covered in this lesson. The introduction in dictionaries explains the symbols and abbreviations used in the entries. Most dictionaries have a chart that explains every possible part of a dictionary entry. Look at the notes and chart in the introduction to help you understand parts of an entry.

Lesson Review Read each entry carefully. Write on your paper the answers to the questions.

> **con•fet•ti** (kən fet´ ē)   *n.* [It. pl. of *confetto,* sweetmeat] bits of colored paper or ribbon for throwing around at celebrations.

1) How many syllables does the word *confetti* have?

2) What vowel sound do you hear in the first syllable?

3) What part of speech is the word *confetti*?

4) What country is the word from?

5) What would you do with confetti?

> **in•voice** (in´vois), *n.* [prob. <MF *envois* messages] a list of goods shipped to a buyer stating prices. – *v.t.* **in•voiced, invoic•ing** to present an invoice for goods sold or services provided to someone.

6) Can *invoice* be used as a verb?

7) What did the word *invoice* mean in Middle French? How was it spelled?

8) When would you expect to get an invoice?

> **e•mo•tion•al** (i mō´shən əl), *adj.* [< L *e-* out + *movere* to move]   **1.** showing strong feeling.   **2.** appealing to the emotions. – **e•mo•tion•al•ly** *adv.*

9) What is the meaning of the word *emotional* in these sentences—meaning 1 or meaning 2?
   a) That music is very emotional.
   b) Marie gets emotional at sad movies.

10) From what language is the word *emotional* derived?

11) How many syllables are in the word *emotional*?

12) What is the adverb form of the word *emotional*?

Even the best spellers need to check the spelling of a word now and then. The dictionary is a useful tool when you want to find out how a word is spelled. You may wonder how you can look up a word if you can't spell it. In this lesson, you will learn some general spelling rules that will help you spell words. You can use the dictionary to check that you have spelled the words correctly.

Spelling the Plurals of Nouns

Form the plural of most nouns by adding -s or -es.

EXAMPLES   house—houses   shoe—shoes

boy—boys   watch—watches

If a noun does not follow the -s or -es rule for forming its plural, look at the dictionary entry to find its plural form.

EXAMPLE

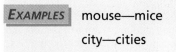

child (child) *n. pl.* **chil•dren** [ME>OE *cild*] **1.** a young girl or boy between the age of infancy and teens. *adj.* childlike.

Here are some other nouns that do not follow the -s or -es rule.

EXAMPLES   mouse—mice   woman—women

city—cities   deer—deer

Activity A   Look up each of the words below in a dictionary. Write the plural form on your paper. Beside each word, write *Yes* if the word follows the -s or -es rule. Write *No* if it does not.

1) dictionary   **5)** moose
2) umbrella   **6)** guess
3) man   **7)** puppy
4) shelf   **8)** key

Adding Endings to Words

Double the final consonant of some words before adding an ending. If you are not sure whether to double the final consonant before adding an ending, check your dictionary.

EXAMPLES	stop	+	ed	=	stopped
	run	+	ing	=	running
	plant	+	ed	=	planted

For some words that end with a silent *e*, drop the *e* before adding an ending. If you are not sure whether to drop the final *e*, check your dictionary.

EXAMPLE

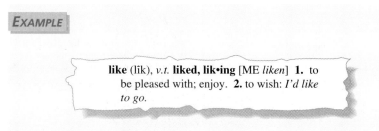

like (līk), *v.t.* **liked, lik•ing** [ME *liken*] **1.** to be pleased with; enjoy. **2.** to wish: *I'd like to go.*

Activity B   Add the endings in parentheses to these words. Write the words with the endings on your paper. Then use a dictionary to check your spelling.

1) bake (ed)

2) charge (ing)

3) use (ful)

4) safe (ty)

5) write (er)

6) step (ing)

7) tall (est)

8) plan (ed)

9) hum (ing)

10) drop (ed)

Spelling Verbs

Add -*ed* to the end of regular verbs to make their past or past participle forms.

> **EXAMPLE** | I walk.   I walk**ed**.   I have walk**ed**.
>
> He fishes.   He fish**ed**.   He has fish**ed**.

Form the past or past participle of irregular verbs in other ways. The dictionary entry will show you the past and, sometimes, the past participle for irregular verb forms, along with the present participle. Study the example.

EXAMPLE

> **sell** (sel), *v.t.* **sold, selling** [ME>OE *sellan* to give, sell] **1.** to turn over to another for a price.

Activity C   Write on your paper the answers to the questions about the entries below.

> **catch** (kach), *v.t.* **caught, catch•ing** [L *capere* take] to capture or take.
>
> **cost** (kost), *v.t.* **cost, cost•ing** [L *constare,* to stand firm] to have a price of.
>
> **creep** (krēp), *v.i.* **crept, creep•ing** [ME *crepen*] to move along with the body close to the ground.
>
> **draw** (drô), *v.t.* **drew, drawn, draw•ing** [ME *drawen*] **1.** to pull: *to draw in a horse.* **2.** to make lines or pictures.
>
> **en•joy** (en joi´), v.t. [ME *enjoyen* to make joyful] to take pleasure in. —**en•joy•a•ble** *adj.* —**en•joy•ment** *n.*

1) Which verb forms its past form in a regular way? How do you know?

2) Which verb does not add an ending to make the past form?

3) Which entry shows four different forms for the verb?

4) Write the past form of *creep.*

Activity D   Write on your paper the past form of the verb in parentheses. Then check your spelling in the entries on page 44.

1) Eddie (draw) a picture in art class.

2) The turtle (creep) across the road.

3) That car (cost) them a lot!

4) Lisa (enjoy) the movie.

Homonyms and Sound-Alike Words

Homonym

A word that sounds exactly like another word but is spelled differently and has a different meaning.

Homonyms are words that sound exactly alike but are spelled differently and have different meanings. To be sure you have used the correct homonym in a sentence, check its meaning and spelling in a dictionary.

> EXAMPLES   there   their   they're
>
> **There** is my house. (adverb)
>
> **Their** vacation starts soon. (pronoun)
>
> **They're** my best friends. (They are)

Words that sound almost alike can also cause spelling problems. To be sure you have used the correct word in a sentence, look up both words in the dictionary. Read the meanings to find out which word you need.

> EXAMPLES   probable   probably
>
> It is **probable** that it will rain today. (adjective)
>
> It will **probably** rain today. (adverb)
>
> accept   except
>
> I am pleased to **accept** this award. (verb)
>
> Everyone was surprised **except** me! (preposition)

Activity E   Write on your paper the word that completes each sentence correctly. Use the dictionary entries to be sure you have used the correct word.

> **its** (its) *pron.* of or relating to it. (used as an adjective)
>
> **it's** (its) **1.** a contraction of *it is.* **2.** a contraction of *it has.*

1) Here is my book. Have you seen _____ cover?

2) _____ been a nice day today.

3) I wonder what _____ name is.

4) _____ a quarter past two.

Other Troublesome Words to Spell

Some words are harder to spell than other words. It may take more than one try to check the spelling of these words in a dictionary.

EXAMPLES

Words with the letters *ei* and *ie* can be tricky.
    reins   science   believe   friend

Words with double consonants are often hard to spell.
    committee   recommend   different

Some words have letters that are not pronounced.
    knowledge   thorough   Wednesday

Some words are pronounced incorrectly and then spelled the way they are pronounced.
    interesting   height   across

Some words are not spelled the way they sound.
    scissors   necessary

Some words sound as if they could begin with different letters.
    eighty   imagine   invite

Activity F   Write on your paper the word that names each picture below. Check the spelling of each word in a dictionary.

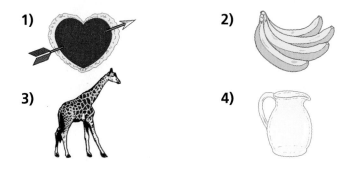

1)

2)

3)

4)

Activity G   Use a dictionary to help you find five spelling errors in the paragraph below. Write the correct spellings on your paper.

Next Munday, I'll call my freind after school. I'll invite him to visit me and my fammily for the weekend. We always find the same things intresting, witch is why we like each other's company.

Part A   The words in bold in the paragraph below are spelled incorrectly. Use a dictionary to find each correct spelling. Write the paragraph on your paper with all of the words spelled correctly.

> The **Basball** Hall of Fame is in Cooperstown, New York. It was **dedecated** in 1939. People like to visit the **musuem**. The Hall of Fame is called "The shrine of **orgonized** baseball." A shrine is a **wholly** place!

Part B   Ten of the words in bold below are misspelled. Check the spelling of all the bold words in a dictionary. Write the misspelled words correctly on your paper.

1) The **foremans** on Robert's job have a meeting every **Wensday**.

2) A friend of mine has two **calfs** for sale.

3) Maria's club **planed** the **Thanxsgiving** party.

4) "Is all that noise **nessessary**?" asked Mr. Williams.

5) "I'm **to** tired for this **comotion**!" he said.

6) Chris would rather see a movie **than** watch TV.

7) "Where is **your** homework?" asked the teacher.

8) He **beleives** that everyone deserves a chance to **suceed**.

You can use a dictionary to find out interesting and important facts. Here are some kinds of facts you might find in a dictionary.

- Facts about real people
- Facts about fictional characters
- Facts about cities, rivers, states, and countries
- The meaning of foreign words

EXAMPLE

Columbus, Christopher. 1451–1506. Italian, served Spain as an explorer. First European to discover America (1492) in an attempt to sail to Asia from Europe.

Activity A Look up the following words in a dictionary. Write on your paper one fact you learn about each item. If your dictionary does not contain an entry for a word, write *no entry* on your paper. Later, look up the word in a different dictionary.

1) hors d'oeuvres

2) Dakota

3) Marconi

4) Robinson Crusoe

5) impressionism

6) pomegranate

7) otter

8) Nike

9) NASA

10) O'Keeffe

Different Kinds of Dictionaries

Most libraries have many different types of dictionaries in the reference section.

Some dictionaries provide special information.

A **geographical dictionary** has a list of rivers, mountains, cities, and other geographical features of the world. A **biographical dictionary** has a list of famous people and some facts about their lives.

A dictionary of synonyms and **antonyms** has a list of words with other words that have the same meanings and words that have opposite meanings.

Activity B   Write on your paper the type of dictionary that would probably have the information listed in each item below. Write *geographical, biographical,* or *synonyms and antonyms.*

1) Information about your town or city

2) A word that means the same as *nice*

3) The date that Calvin Coolidge became president

4) A word that means the opposite of *large*

5) A list of some of the inventions of Thomas Edison

6) The height of Mount Everest

Geographical dictionary

A reference book with a list of rivers, mountains, cities, and other features.

Biographical dictionary

A reference book that lists famous people and facts about their lives.

Antonym

A word that means the opposite of another word.

Find the answers
to these questions
in a dictionary.

1. What color is a topaz?

2. Where would you be likely to see a llama?

3. Was Hercules a real person?

4. Marie's teacher said that Marie was loquacious. What other word might the teacher have used to describe Marie?

5. Where is the Mojave Desert?

6. What would you do with a glockenspiel?

7. When did people do the jitterbug?

Activity C Use the information in the entries below to complete this activity. Write your answers on your paper.

au gra·tin (ō grät´ən), *adj.* [F *with scrapings*] made with a crust of bread crumbs and cheese.

Ba·con (bā´kən), *n.* **Francis,** 1561–1626, English philosopher and writer.

ba·gel (bā´ gəl), *n.* [Yiddish] a hard bread roll shaped like a small doughnut.

Bagh·dad (bag´ dad), *n.* capital city of Iraq; pop. about 1,000,000. also **Bagdad.**

ban·shee (ban´ shē), *n.* (in Irish folklore) a female spirit whose loud screams warn of a coming death.

bant·am·weight (bant´ əm wāt), *n.* a boxer or wrestler weighing 113 to 118 pounds.

Bar·num (bär´ nəm), *n.* P(hineas) T(aylor), 1810–91, U.S. showman and circus owner.

chop su·ey (chop sōō´ ē), *n.* a Chinese-American dish of meat, bean sprouts, etc., served with rice.

C.O.D. *abbr.* **1.** cash on delivery. **2.** collect on delivery.

dè·já vu (dā zhä vyōo), n. [F *already seen*] the feeling that one has previously had an experience that is actually new.

Doyle (doil), *n.* **Sir Arthur Conan** (kō´nən), 1859–1930, British physician and novelist: known for his Sherlock Holmes stories.

flib·ber·ti·gib·bet (flib´ ər tə jib´ it), *n.* an irresponsible flighty person.

leap year *n.* a year of 366 days, occurring every fourth year; the extra day is on February 29: a leap year is a year whose number can be divided by 4.

L.P.N. *abbr.* licensed practical nurse.

Mickey Mouse *adj.* [a tradename for a cartoon character created by Walt Disney] lacking importance, unrelated to reality: *a Mickey Mouse course.*

pop. (pop) *abbr.* **1.** popular. **2.** population.

R.N. *abbr.* **1.** registered nurse. **2.** Royal Navy.

Sher·lock Holmes (shûr´ lok hōmz´), *n.* a fictional British detective with great powers of deduction, the main character in many stories by A. Conan Doyle.

Yo·sem·i·te Falls (yō sem´ ə tē), *n.* [AmInd name of the Valley Indians, lit. *grizzly bears, killers*] series of waterfalls in Yosemite National Park in California: upper falls, 1,430 ft.; lower falls, 320 ft.; total drop: 2,526 ft.

a - act, ā - āble, â - dâre, ä - ärm, e - ebb, ē - ēven, i - it, ī - īce,
o - hot, ō - ōver, ô - ôrder, oi - oil, ŏŏ - bŏŏk, ōō - lōōt, ou - out,
u - up, û - ûrge, ch - chief, ng - sing, sh - shoe, th - thin, th - this,
zh - vision,   ə = a as in *ago.*

1) List the entries that are foreign words.

2) List the names of real people.

3) List the fictional characters.

4) List the entries that are abbreviations. Write what they mean.

5) List the geographical locations.

Activity D   Use the information in the entries on page 51 to answer these questions. Write the answers in complete sentences on your paper.

1) Burt weighs 119 pounds. Can he wrestle as a bantamweight?

2) Chris wants to become an L.P.N. What does the *L* stand for?

3) The movie the children saw starred Mickey Mouse. Was the leading character in the movie real?

4) Aunt Margaret ordered spinach au gratin. What did the cook put on the spinach?

5) Who is the real person—Sherlock Holmes or Arthur Conan Doyle?

6) What is the translation of *Yosemite*?

7) What are two ways to spell the name of the capital of Iraq?

8) Describe a bagel.

9) "Stop being a flibbertigibbet!" Aunt Margaret said to Eddie. Why would Eddie's aunt say this?

10) Mrs. Gomez received a package C.O.D. What did she have to do?

Lesson Review   Use the entries to answer the questions that follow. Write the answers on your paper.

Ak•ron (ak´ rən), *n.* a city in N.E. Ohio: pop. 275,425.

Al•ex•an•der the Great (al´ ig zan´ dər), 356–323 B.C.; king of Macedonia, 336–323; conqueror.

an•cient (ān´ shənt), *adj.* [< L *ante* before] **1.** of times long past. **2.** very old.

At•lan•tis (at lan´ tis), *n.* a mythical island in the Atlantic Ocean west of Gibralter, and that was swallowed up by the sea.

B.C. *abbr.* **1.** bachelor of commerce. **2.** before Christ. **3.** British Columbia.

e•qui•nox (ē´ kwə noks´), *n.* [< L *aequus* equal + *nox* night] the time when the sun crosses the equator, making night and day an equal length in all parts of the earth.

Leip•zig (līp´ sig), *n.* a city in Germany; pop. 596,000.

N. *abbr.* **1.** north. **2.** northern.

---

1) Which city has more people—Akron or Leipzig?

2) Was Alexander the Great a real person? How do you know?

3) Twice each year, day and night are equal in Norway. Are they equal on these same days where you live?

4) When Vanessa's brother graduates from college, he will receive a B.C. degree. What do those letters mean?

5) Lynda's parents live in B.C. What is the full name of that place?

6) How old was Alexander the Great when he became king of Macedonia?

7) Can tourists visit the island of Atlantis?

Part A   Write the answers to these questions on your paper.

1) Where are the guide words found in a dictionary?

2) Here are two guide words: fancy—fashion
   a) What is the first entry on this page?
   b) What is the last entry on this page?
   c) Would you find the entry *family* on this page?

3) Where do you usually find a pronunciation key?

4) Which part of the entry does the pronunciation key explain?

5) What does each of these abbreviations or symbols mean?
   a) v.i.   **c)** adj.   **e)** pl.
   b) pop.   **d)** <   **f)** L

Part B   Use the entry below to answer the questions that follow. Write the answers on your paper.

> **com•pas•sion**   (kəm pãsh´ ən), n. [ME>L. *compati,* to suffer, bear pain. See PATIENT.] **1.** the feeling of another's pain or sorrow. **Syn.** pity, concern

1) How many syllables does *compassion* have?

2) What part of speech is *compassion*?

3) What is the origin of *compassion*?

4) What other word could you look up to find information about the origin of *compassion*?

5) Do people with *compassion* care about others' feelings?

Part C   Check the spelling of each word in bold in a dictionary. Then number your paper from 1 to 5. Beside each number, copy the word if it is spelled correctly. If the word in bold is misspelled, write the word correctly.

1) I **beleive** that he has lived in five different **citys**.

2) The **safety** of the **childrens** was her biggest concern.

3) She **catched** the ball for the final out, and **evryone** cheered.

4) My sisters are coming, but **there probably** going to be late.

5) It was **nessessary** for the winner to **except** the prize in person.

Part D   Use the entries below to answer the questions that follow. Write the answers on your paper.

> **John•son** (jon´sən), *n.* **1. Andrew** 1808-75; 17th president of the U.S. 1865-69. **2. James Weldon** (wel´ dən), 1871-1938; U.S. writer. **3. Lyn•don Baines** (lin´ dən bānz), 1908-73; 36th U.S. president 1963-69. **4. Samuel** 1709-84; Eng. lexicographer and writer.
>
> **lex•i•cog•ra•pher** (lek´ sə kog´rə fər), *n.* a person who writes a dictionary.
>
> **Lou•is** (loo´ is), **Joe** (born *Joseph Louis Barrow*) 1914-81; U.S. boxer: world heavyweight champion 1937-49.
>
> **Lou•is•ville** (loo´ ē vil´), *n.* (after Louis XVI) city in Northern Kentucky on the Ohio river: pop. 361,958.
>
> **par•a•dise** (par´ ə dīs´), *n.* [< Gk *paradeisos* garden] **1.** the garden of Eden. **2.** heaven. **3.** any place of great happiness.

1) How many U.S. presidents were named Johnson?

2) Who was James Weldon Johnson?

3) What kind of book does a lexicographer write?

4) Who was the city of Louisville named after?

5) What are two meanings of *paradise?*

| Test Taking Tip | Use a marker to highlight important facts and terms in your notes. Review the highlighted areas before the test. |

Some Everyday References

H ave you ever needed to know how to fix a leaky faucet? Make a special dessert? Or get to a place you wanted to visit? Books, magazines, and other references can help you find the answers you are looking for. You just need to know which reference has the information you need and where to find the reference. Then you need to know how to use the information you found.

In Chapter 3, you will learn how to find and use everyday references.

Goals for Learning

▶ To discover the kinds of information in an almanac

▶ To understand and use the contents of an atlas

▶ To locate information in an encyclopedia

▶ To follow directions in a recipe

▶ To follow directions in a how-to book

▶ To recognize and find different kinds of information in magazines

Lesson 1 What's in an Almanac?

An almanac is a book of facts published once a year. Two kinds of almanacs are farmer's almanacs and general information almanacs. Some almanacs are published on **CD-ROM**. CD-ROM stands for compact disc read-only memory. You use a computer to find the information in almanacs on CD-ROM.

CD-ROM

A computer science term that stands for compact disc read-only memory.

Farmer's Almanacs

A **farmer's almanac** is a yearly calendar of days, weeks, and months with weather forecasts and facts about astronomy. The weather forecasts help farmers decide when to plant or harvest crops. Because the moon affects tides, mariners use the astronomy information in farmer's almanacs to determine when the tide will be high or low. Farmer's almanacs provide other information helpful for farm and home management.

Farmer's almanac

An annual calendar of days, weeks, and months with weather predictions and astronomical facts.

Phases of the Moon

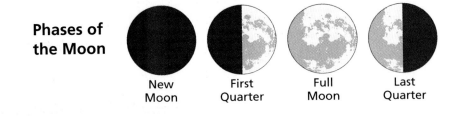

New Moon   First Quarter   Full Moon   Last Quarter

USING WHAT YOU HAVE LEARNED

1. Find a farmer's almanac in a library and study it.
2. Look up *new moon* and *full moon* in a dictionary.
3. The Latin word for *moon* has another meaning. Can you guess what it is? Check a dictionary.

Activity A   Write the answers to these questions on your paper.

1) Would you expect to find a calendar in a farmer's almanac?

2) Why would a ship's navigator want to know about the phases of the moon?

3) Name two kinds of information that are in farmer's almanacs.

General Information Almanacs

A **general information almanac** has facts and figures about many subjects from the most recent year and from the past. Most general information almanacs are published once a year. Two popular general information almanacs are *The World Almanac and Book of Facts* and *The Information Please Almanac*. To discover what topics an almanac covers, look in the index. Unlike most other reference books, the index of an almanac is usually in the front of the book.

Here are some topics you might find in a general information almanac:

Biographies of U.S. presidents	Agricultural facts
Facts about the United States	Awards and prizes
Facts about other countries	Events of the last year
Facts about Social Security	History of the world
Number of calories in foods	Income tax information
Populations of U.S. cities	Names of U.S. colleges
Supreme Court decisions	People in Congress
ZIP codes and area codes	Sports facts

Activity B Write complete sentences on your paper to answer these questions.

1) How is the index in an almanac different from indexes in other reference works?

2) What are three types of facts you might find in a general information almanac?

3) A statistic is a numerical fact. Write three statistics from this almanac account:

> William Henry Harrison was the ninth president of the United States. He was president only 31 days. He got pneumonia during the inauguration and died on April 4, 1841.

An almanac can be very useful in your everyday life; for example:

- if you are on a special diet, you can find facts about calories and nutrition.

- if you want information about a college, you can find the names, addresses, number of students, and number of teachers in most of the colleges and universities in the United States.

- if you are interested in sports, you can find facts about nearly every sport and sporting event.

- if you are writing a letter, most almanacs list the ZIP codes for each area of the United States.

- if you have purchased a product that doesn't work, you can find the addresses of many large companies.

- if you are interested in choosing a career with plenty of job openings, almanacs list the most rapidly expanding careers.

- if you want information about recent world events, almanacs list that information.

An almanac has facts about the year *before* its title date. For example, the 1997 almanac includes facts about 1996. To learn facts about 1997, you would have to read the 1998 almanac.

To find information that is more current, use a publication that is issued more often. For instance, magazines come out every week or every month. The most up-to-date facts are in the daily newspaper.

Activity C   Use these facts from an almanac published in 1995 to answer the questions that follow. Write your answers on your paper.

1995 Almanac

Awards — Medals — Prizes

<u>1994 Nobel Prize Winners</u>

Physics	Bertram N. Brockhouse, Canada
	Clifford G. Shull, U.S.
Chemistry	George A. Olah, U.S.
Physiology/Medicine	Alfred G. Golman, U.S.
	Martin Rodbell, U.S.

<u>1994 Nobel Prize Winners</u>

Literature	Kenzaburo Oe, Japan
Peace	Yasir Arafat, Palestine
	Shimon Peres, Israel
	Yitzhak Rabin, Israel

<u>Pulitzer Prize in Journalism, Letters, & Music</u>

Journalism

1995	Virgin Islands Daily News, St. Thomas
1994	Akron Beacon Journal
1993	Miami Herald

<u>Miss America Winners</u>

1996	Shawntel Smith, Muldrow, Oklahoma
1995	Heather Whitestone, Birmingham, Alabama
1994	Kimberly Aiken, Columbia, South Carolina

<u>Academy Awards 1994</u>

Best Picture	*Forrest Gump*
Best Actor	Tom Hanks, *Forrest Gump*
Best Actress	Jessica Lange, *Blue Sky*
Best Director	Robert Zemeckis, *Forrest Gump*

123

1) Where did the winner of the 1994 Nobel Prize in literature come from? What was that person's name?

2) What countries were represented by the 1994 Nobel Peace Prize winners?

3) What was the top picture of 1994? How do you know that?

4) Who is Heather Whitestone?

5) What newspaper won the Pulitzer Prize in Journalism in 1995?

Part A   Write complete sentences on your paper to answer these questions.

1) What are two kinds of information given in a farmer's almanac?

2) What kinds of facts would you find in a general information almanac? Give two examples.

3) Name one popular general information almanac.

4) How often are most almanacs published?

5) Where would you look first to find out if an almanac has information about a certain country?

6) What is a statistic?

Part B   Number your paper from 1 to 8. Beside each number write *FA* if you can find the answer to the question in a farmer's almanac or *GIA* if you can find the answer to the question in a general information almanac.

1) When will the next full moon be?

2) Suppose that the fish are biting best at high tide. What time should you go fishing?

3) Who won the World Series in 1950?

4) When should I set out my tomato plants this year?

5) Who won the Oscar for best actor in 1993?

6) What is the ZIP code for Boise, Idaho?

7) Which team won the Super Bowl in 1995?

8) What would be the best day to plant my garden this year?

Atlas

A book of maps and geographical facts.

Gazetteer

A dictionary of geographical place names.

Scale

The relationship shown between distances on the map and actual distances.

Symbol

A sign or mark that stands for something else.

An **atlas** is a book of maps. A **gazetteer** is a dictionary of geographical place names. Both of these reference sources can also be found on CD-ROM.

In Greek mythology, there was a Titan named Atlas. Titans were a family of giants who wanted to rule the heavens. When Zeus defeated the Titans, Zeus punished Atlas by making him hold the Earth and sky on his shoulders forever. For hundreds of years, books of maps have shown a drawing of Atlas holding up the earth. As a result, people began to call any book of maps an "atlas."

Reading a Map

To use an atlas, you must be able to read a map. To read a map, you must understand its symbols. A **symbol** is something that represents something else. The key, or legend, on a map explains the symbols used on the map.

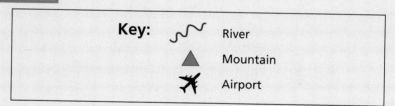

Maps are drawn to **scale**. You can use the scale to find the actual distances shown on the map.

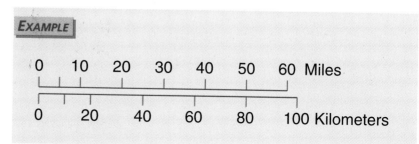

Activity A Use the map below to answer the questions that follow. Write the answers on your paper.

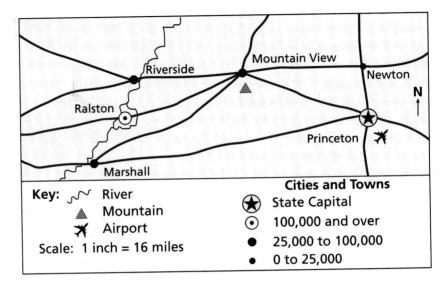

Key: River
∆ Mountain
✈ Airport
Scale: 1 inch = 16 miles

Cities and Towns
⭐ State Capital
⊙ 100,000 and over
● 25,000 to 100,000
● 0 to 25,000

1) How far is the mountain from the river?

2) Which city is the capital?

3) If this map shows all of Gilbert County, how wide is the county from east to west?

4) What city has a population of 100,000 or more?

5) What town has fewer than 25,000 people?

Kinds of Maps

There are many different kinds of maps with different features and purposes. Here are some kinds of maps.

Globe

A model of the earth. It shows the actual placement of the continents, islands, and oceans.

Physical map

A map that shows the roughness of the earth's surface.

Political map

A map that shows the boundaries of states and countries clearly.

Product map

A map that has symbols that show where goods are grown or produced.

Road map

A map that shows roads, highways, towns, and other useful travel information.

Road map:	Shows roads, highways, towns, and other information helpful to a traveler.
Political map:	Shows the boundaries of states and countries clearly. Usually each state or country is in a different color.
Physical map:	Shows the roughness of the earth's surface. Mountains and hills can be seen, along with rivers.
Globe:	A model of the earth. It shows the placement of the continents, islands, and oceans as they actually are.
Product map:	Uses symbols to show where goods are grown or produced.

Activity B Match each of the maps below to one of the descriptions above. Then number your paper from 1–4. Beside each number, write the kind of map shown.

1)

2)

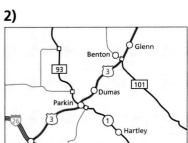

3) 4)

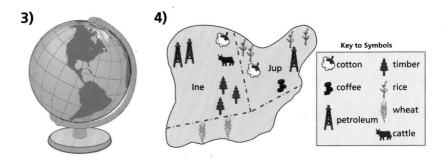

How to Use a Gazetteer

A gazetteer is a dictionary of geographical place names. It is like an index. It lists the names of all the places shown on the maps in the atlas in alphabetical order.

A **grid** is a network of lines on a map that helps to locate certain places. The lines go across (**horizontal**) and up and down (**vertical**). A **grid map** is a map with grid lines. The spaces between the vertical lines on a grid map have numbers. The spaces between the horizontal lines have letters.

The letter and number beside a place name in the gazetteer tells you exactly where to look on the map to locate that place.

Grid

A network of lines on a map that makes it possible to locate specific places.

Grid map

A map with grid lines.

Horizontal

A word that means going across.

Vertical

A word that means going up and down.

EXAMPLE If you were to look up Etonville in the gazetteer of the atlas for this map, you might see:

Etonville B-4

To locate Etonville on the map, first find the B down the left or right side of the map. Then find the 4 across the top or bottom of the map. Run your finger across the map from the B to the space under the 4. Etonville is located in the square beside the B and under the 4.

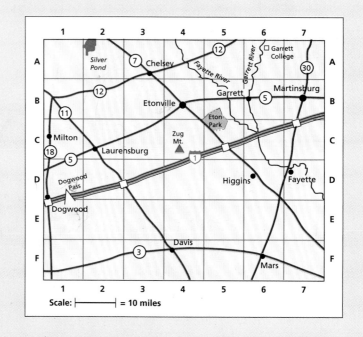

Activity C   Locate each place listed in the gazetteer below on the map on page 66.

Dogwood D-1

Fayette River A-4, B-5, C-6, D-7

Laurensburg C-2

Martinsburg B-7

Zug Mountain C-4

Mars E-6

Activity D   Locate each of these places on the map on page 66. On your paper, write the letter and number of their location on the grid.

1) Milton

2) Garrett River

3) Dogwood Pass

4) Higgins

5) Chelsey

6) Eton Park

7) Silver Pond

8) Garrett College

9) Fayette

10) Davis

Activity E   Use the map on page 66 to answer these questions. Write the answers on your paper.

1) What road connects Milton and Dogwood?

2) How far is it from Silver Pond to Chelsey?

3) Which town is closer to Zug Mountain—Laurensburg or Etonville?

4) How far is Martinsburg from Garrett College?

5) What town is next to the Garrett River?

6) What towns are located along Route 7?

Study this sample classroom map. Then complete the activity below.

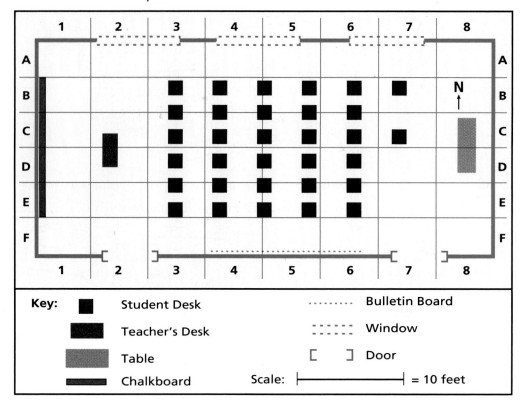

Activity F Draw a grid map of your classroom on your paper. Create a map key. Use the symbols shown in the sample map above or make up some of your own.

Longitude and Latitude

A globe is a model of the earth. Like the earth, a globe is a round object. Mapmakers have divided the surface of the globe into parts. They use imaginary lines called longitude and latitude.

Longitude lines go from north to south (vertically) on a map. They are used to measure the distance from east to west. **Latitude lines** go from east to west (horizontally) on a map. They are used to measure the distance from north to south.

Equator

An imaginary line that circles the center of the earth.

The **equator** is an imaginary line of latitude. It runs from east to west around the center of the earth. All other lines of latitude are measured from the equator.

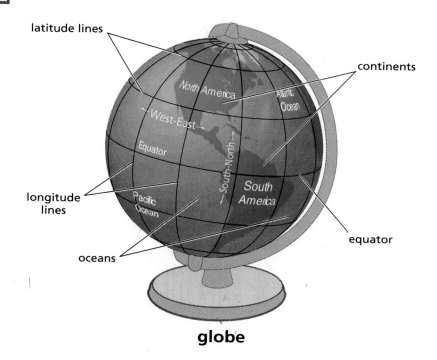

globe

Activity G   Use the view of the globe above to answer these questions. Write the answers on your paper.

1) What is the name of the latitude line in the center of the globe?

2) What two continents are shown on the globe?

3) Which continent is mostly south of the equator?

4) What two bodies of water are shown on the globe?

5) Which body of water is west of the two continents?

Part A Use the sample classroom map on page 68 to answer these questions. Write the answers on your paper.

1) If you are sitting at the teacher's desk facing the classroom, what direction are you facing?
2) How many windows does the classroom have?
3) How wide (in feet) is each window?
4) What classroom object is located between the two doors?
5) If you are looking out one of the windows, what direction are you facing?
6) What is directly behind the teacher's desk?

Part B Create a gazetteer on your paper for the classroom map on page 68. Include the items listed below. Remember that the items in a gazetteer are listed in alphabetical order.

Example Bulletin board   F-4, 5, 6

1) West door
2) East door
3) Middle window

4) Teacher's desk
5) Chalkboard
6) Table

Part C Write on your paper the name of the place found at each of these locations on the grid map below.

1) C-4
2) A-2

3) B-1
4) D-1

5) D-5
6) C-2

7) A-4
8) D-3

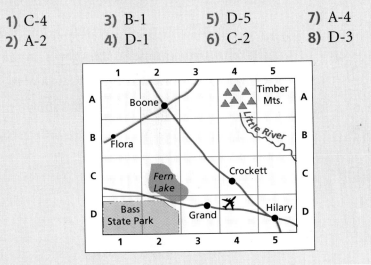

Encyclopedia

A book or set of books with a collection of articles and facts on many subjects, organized in alphabetical order.

Encyclopedia

A book or set of books with a collection of articles and facts on many subjects, organized in alphabetical order.

Volume

A single book, or one book in a set of books.

A very useful type of reference book is an **encyclopedia**. An encyclopedia is a book or set of books with facts on many subjects. It is usually a collection of articles in alphabetical order.

Some encyclopedias are only one book, or **volume**. Others are a set of books, or volumes. *The World Book Encyclopedia,* the *Encyclopædia Brittanica,* and *Compton's Encyclopedia* all have many volumes. Most sets of encyclopedias have similar features, as shown in the diagram below. These features can help you find the information you need quickly.

Inside each volume, guide words appear at the top of each page.

Guide letters often appear on each volume.

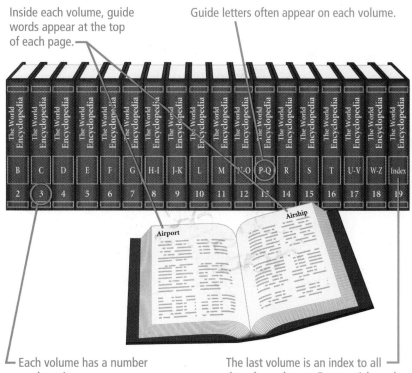

Each volume has a number on the spine.

The last volume is an index to all the other volumes. Every article and subject in the encyclopedia is listed. Cross references are often given.

Encyclopedias are also on CD-ROM. These encyclopedias present information, such as videos and music recordings, in a way that cannot be presented in books.

Activity A Which volume of the encyclopedia pictured on page 71 would you look in to find facts about each topic listed below? Since some topics may suggest more than one idea, write the volume number or numbers on your paper. Beside each number, write the subject you would look up.

Example Honeysuckle plants
Vol. 8—honeysuckle
Vol. 13—plants

1) History of Argentina

2) Fish of North America

3) Animals of the Amazon rain forest

4) United States history

5) Basketball

6) Products of Mexico

7) Benjamin Franklin's inventions

8) Robin Hood

9) The Supreme Court

Related Topics and Cross-References

When you read about a topic in an encyclopedia, you may find that the article names another related topic. Some articles also give a specific cross-reference to another related topic. If you look up these related topics, you will find more information about your subject.

HONEY PLANTS, a group of plants that furnish the nectar from which bees make honey — often also called bee plants.

NECTAR is a sugary liquid produced by many flowers. Besides being the main source of honey, it is also very important in cross-pollination. *See also* **Pollination**. G.W.K.

When you use a CD-ROM encyclopedia, you click on a part of the computer screen to see cross-references. When you use books, you may have to refer to another volume of the encyclopedia.

Activity B Use the encyclopedia entries on page 72 to answer these questions. Write the answers on your paper.

1) What is the related topic named in the entry about honey plants?
2) If you were to look up this topic, what guide letter would appear on the correct volume?
3) What is the cross-reference named in the article on nectar?
4) What do you think the letters G. W. K. refer to at the end of the entry on nectar?
5) Where might you look to find out what those letters mean?
6) What is another name for honey plants?
7) What guide letter would appear on the volume containing the article about pollination?
8) Would the article about honey plants be on a page with these guide words: Harrisburg—Honduras?

Activity C Use the examples below to answer the questions that follow. Write the answers on your paper.

Example 1

... Boundary arguments with Guatemala were settled in 1933. For Bibliography, *See* Costa Rica (History).

Example 2

HONDURAS, BRITISH. *See* Belize (History).
HONDURAS BARK is the bitter bark from a small tropical American shrub, used as a medicine. Also called Cascarilla Bark.

1) What two specific cross-references are named in the examples above?
2) What related topic would you look up to learn more about Honduras bark?
3) What is a bibliography? Use a dictionary if you need to.
4) The article in *Example 1* has a bibliography. What topic must you look up to find it?
5) Explain what Costa Rica (History) means.
6) What will be the guide letter on the volume that contains the articles in *Example 2*?
7) What will be the guide letter on the volume that has a related article about British Honduras?

Encyclopedias About Special Subjects

You are probably most familiar with the large sets of encyclopedias. However, there are many other kinds of encyclopedias. One-volume general encyclopedias have short articles about many different subjects. They are sometimes called "desk" encyclopedias. One example is the *Columbia Encyclopedia*.

There are also encyclopedias about just one subject. In these encyclopedias, all the articles provide details about that subject. For example, a home medical encyclopedia includes only information related to medical topics.

Activity D   Write the word on your paper that completes each sentence correctly.

1) An encyclopedia is a collection of _____ on many subjects.

2) The subjects in an encyclopedia are arranged in _____ order.

3) The last volume of a set of encyclopedias is often an _____.

4) The topics in an index are arranged in _____ order.

5) An index is to an encyclopedia as a gazetteer is to an _____

6) A desk encyclopedia has _____ volume.

7) A _____ is one in a set of books.

8) A _____ tells where to look to find information on a related topic.

9) You may find the author's _____ at the end of an article in an encyclopedia.

Part A Write the answer to these questions on your paper.

1) What is one way that dictionaries and encyclopedias are alike?

2) What is one way that almanacs and encyclopedias are alike?

3) What is one difference between a desk encyclopedia and *The World Book Encyclopedia?*

4) Encyclopedia sets have guide letters on the spine of each volume. What else may appear there to help you find the right volume?

5) What do the guide words on each page tell you?

Part B Study the encyclopedia in the picture. In which volume would you look to find each topic below? Write the number and the guide letters of the volume on your paper.

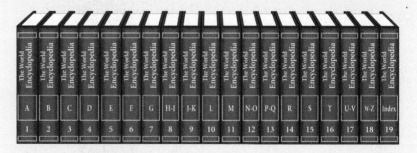

1) President Franklin Roosevelt

2) The History of France

3) The Solar System

4) Football (History)

5) Cities of Saudi Arabia

6) Wildlife of Australia

7) Alexander the Great

8) Zebras

Cookbooks

A cookbook is a reference book about food. Most cookbooks contain some of the following information:

- Facts about storing foods
- Meal planning help
- How to carve meat
- Food shopping advice
- Nutrition facts
- Calorie charts
- Suggestions for a low-fat diet
- How to measure ingredients

There are general cookbooks, such as *Betty Crocker's Picture Cookbook* or the *Good Housekeeping Cookbook.* There are specialty cookbooks like *Cooking With a Wok* or *Simple and Healthy Cooking.*

Activity A   Write *Yes* or *No* on your paper to tell whether a cookbook would have the answer to these questions.

1) How many calories are in a baked potato?
2) How do you carve a turkey?
3) Which store in your town has the best fresh fruit?
4) How can you tell if a watermelon is ripe?
5) What foods are good for breakfast?
6) What should you eat to be sure you get enough vitamins?
7) How do you store fresh vegetables?
8) How can you cook pork chops?
9) How much do blueberries cost?
10) How long should you roast a 15-pound turkey?

Recipe
A list of ingredients and directions for the preparation of a specific food.

A **recipe** is set of directions a cook uses to prepare each part of a meal. Recipes use many specialized terms and abbreviations.

Most cookbooks give the meanings of recipe terms and abbreviations in the front or back of the book. These meanings do not appear in the actual recipe. Here are some of the most common cooking terms and abbreviations.

Terms Used in Cooking	
baste	To brush melted butter or drippings over a food that is cooking.
beat	To mix ingredients until smooth.
blend	To combine two or more ingredients well.
boil	To cook in bubbling hot liquid; 212°F.
braise	To brown meat in hot fat on all sides; then to add liquid, cover, and simmer until tender.
broil	To cook under the heat of a broiler, or directly over hot coals.
cream	To mix sugar and shortening until completely mixed and creamy.
cut into	To use two knives or a pastry blender to cut shortening into dry ingredients until the fat particles are tiny.
dice	To cut into very small cubes.
dissolve	To mix a dry ingredient with liquid until the dry particles disappear.
drain	To pour off the liquid.
ingredient	One of the items that is used in a food mixture.
marinate	To soak a food in a liquid mixture to improve its flavor.
mince	To chop fine.
peel	To cut off the skin from a food, such as a potato or apple.
sauté	To fry a food in a small amount of fat.
shortening	Fat, such as margarine, butter, or lard.
simmer	To cook at a temperature just below boiling.
tender	Easily chewed.
uniform	All the same.

Activity B   Choose the word in parentheses that completes each cooking instruction correctly. Write the word on your paper.

1) (Marinate, Mince) the meat in French dressing for one hour.

2) Boil the carrots for half an hour; then (boil, drain) the water.

3) (Baste, Cream) the sugar and butter in a bowl.

4) Partly cover and (dissolve, simmer) the soup for an hour.

Here are some abbreviations that are used in recipes.

Abbreviations Used in Recipes			
lb.	= pound	min.	= minute
oz.	= ounce	hr.	= hour
doz.	= dozen	pt.	= pint
pkg.	= package	qt.	= quart
tsp.	= teaspoon	F	= Fahrenheit
t.	= teaspoon	g	= gram
tbsp.	= tablespoon	c.	= cup
T.	= tablespoon	sq.	= square

Activity C   Write each underlined term and abbreviation in the recipe below on your paper. Beside each term and abbreviation, write its meaning.

Salsa Cruda

1 16-<u>oz.</u> can of <u>drained</u> and chopped tomatoes
1 4-<u>oz.</u> can of green chili drained, seeded, and <u>diced</u>
1/2 <u>c.</u> of onion, <u>minced</u>
1 <u>T.</u> of vinegar
1 <u>t.</u> of sugar
1/8 <u>tsp.</u> of salt

<u>Blend</u> the following <u>ingredients</u> in a bowl: tomatoes, green chili, and onion. Add vinegar, sugar, and salt to tomato mixture. Keep at room temperature for 30 <u>min.</u> Serve with tacos and enchiladas.

Kitchen Tools

After listing ingredients, most recipes tell you how to prepare those ingredients. For example, a recipe might say "beat 2 eggs well." To follow this instruction, it would be helpful for you to know what kitchen tool you should use to beat eggs.

Here are some common kitchen tools, or utensils, and their uses.

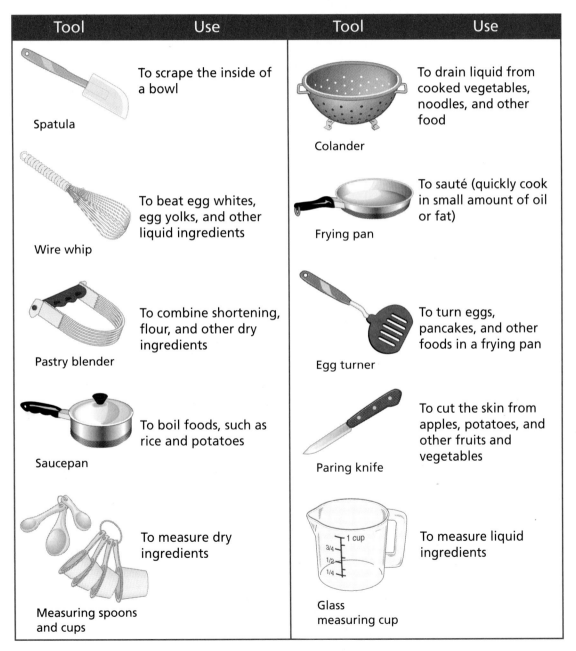

Tool	Use	Tool	Use
Spatula	To scrape the inside of a bowl	Colander	To drain liquid from cooked vegetables, noodles, and other food
Wire whip	To beat egg whites, egg yolks, and other liquid ingredients	Frying pan	To sauté (quickly cook in small amount of oil or fat)
Pastry blender	To combine shortening, flour, and other dry ingredients	Egg turner	To turn eggs, pancakes, and other foods in a frying pan
Saucepan	To boil foods, such as rice and potatoes	Paring knife	To cut the skin from apples, potatoes, and other fruits and vegetables
Measuring spoons and cups	To measure dry ingredients	Glass measuring cup	To measure liquid ingredients

Activity D   Read each recipe below. Then write on your paper the name of the kitchen utensils you could use to prepare each recipe. Beside the name of each utensil, explain how you would use it.

Double-Crust Pie Dough

2 cups all-purpose flour
1 tsp. salt

2/3 cup shortening
5 to 8 tbsp. cold water

Blend together flour and salt. Cut shortening into flour mixture until pea-sized pieces form. Sprinkle with cold water, adding 1 tbsp. at a time. Toss after each tablespoon water is added. When mixture sticks together, shape into a ball. Cut ball into two halves. Roll out each ball to 1/8 inch thickness on lightly floured surface or pastry sheet.

Spaghetti With Tomato Sauce

3 large cloves of garlic
2 tbsp. olive oil
1 can (3 1/3 c.) Italian tomato puree

2 tsp. oregano
salt / pepper
1 lb. spaghetti

Peel and slice garlic. Sauté garlic in olive oil over medium to high heat. Remove garlic. Add tomato puree and oregano. Cook over medium heat for 15 to 20 minutes, stirring occasionally. Add salt and pepper to taste. Meanwhile, bring 4 qts. of water to boil. Add spaghetti and cook according to package directions. Drain cooked spaghetti and serve topped with sauce.

Following a Recipe

Here are some important steps you should follow to be sure that the recipes you prepare turn out right.

Step 1	Read the whole recipe.
Step 2	Assemble all of the ingredients called for in the recipe.
Step 3	Gather all of the utensils you will need.
Step 4	Follow the directions in order.

Activity E Read the recipe below. Then write on your paper the answers to the questions that follow.

Mashed Vegetables

1 lb. medium potatoes
3 large carrots
2 cloves garlic

butter
salt / black pepper
paprika

Peel and slice potatoes. Trim and peel carrots. Cut carrots into chunks. Boil potatoes and carrots with peeled garlic until soft in enough water to cover the vegetables. Drain cooked vegetables. Mash the vegetables with a hand-masher or in a food processor. Add butter, salt, and black pepper to taste. Sprinkle with paprika before serving.

1) What ingredients will you need to prepare this recipe?

2) What utensils will you need?

3) After gathering ingredients and utensils, what is the next thing you must do?

4) What should you do before serving this recipe?

Following Directions on a Package

Packaged foods come in cans, boxes, and sealed plastic bags. Some packaged foods are stored at room temperature. Some are frozen. Packaged foods are convenient. Almost anyone who can read can prepare them. Simple and easy-to-follow recipes are printed on the packages. Use what you have learned about following a recipe to prepare packaged foods.

Activity F   Read these directions from a package of macaroni and cheese. Then write on your paper the answers to the questions that follow.

Directions
Add macaroni and 1 tsp. salt to 6 c. boiling water. Stir. Boil rapidly, stirring occasionally, 7 to 10 minutes or to desired tenderness. Drain. Add 1/4 c. margarine, 1/4 c. milk, and the cheese sauce mix; mix well. Makes 4 1/2 cup servings.

1) Dry macaroni and an envelope of cheese sauce mix were in the box. What other ingredients would you need to prepare this meal?

2) What utensils would you need?

3) What is the first thing you would do if you were following the directions correctly?

4) How long would you cook the macaroni?

5) What would you use to drain the macaroni?

6) What would you do after you drained the macaroni?

7) How large would the servings be if only two people ate this meal?

Preparing Frozen Foods

Frozen vegetables are easy to cook, and they taste good. Freezing keeps more of the vegetable's fresh flavor and nutritional value. Like other packaged food, directions for preparing frozen vegetables are printed on the package.

Activity G   Read these directions from a package of frozen broccoli cuts. Then write on your paper the answers to the questions that follow.

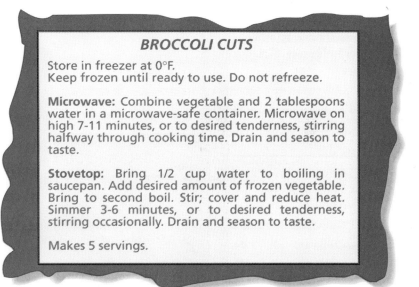

BROCCOLI CUTS

Store in freezer at 0°F.
Keep frozen until ready to use. Do not refreeze.

Microwave: Combine vegetable and 2 tablespoons water in a microwave-safe container. Microwave on high 7-11 minutes, or to desired tenderness, stirring halfway through cooking time. Drain and season to taste.

Stovetop: Bring 1/2 cup water to boiling in saucepan. Add desired amount of frozen vegetable. Bring to second boil. Stir; cover and reduce heat. Simmer 3-6 minutes, or to desired tenderness, stirring occasionally. Drain and season to taste.

Makes 5 servings.

1) Where would you store the package of broccoli?

2) Where would be the best place to store the package if it were to thaw before you were ready to use it?

3) What other ingredients besides broccoli and water would you need to prepare the vegetable?

4) What utensils would you use for each method of cooking?

5) What is the first step of the directions for each method of cooking?

6) Which is the fastest method of cooking the broccoli?

7) How many servings does one package make?

Food Labels

The label on a food package lists all of the package's ingredients in order of **predominance**. That means that the ingredient of the greatest quantity is listed first. The ingredient with the smallest amount is listed last. Labels also give nutrition information per serving.

EXAMPLES

MACARONI & CHEESE DINNER

Nutrition Facts

Serving Size 2.5 oz.
(70g / about 1/3 Box)
(Makes about 1 cup)
Servings Per Container about 3

Amount Per Serving	In Box	Prep
Calories	260	390
Calories from Fat	25	150

	% Daily Value**	
Total Fat 2.5g*	4%	26%
Saturated Fat 1g	5%	20%
Cholesterol 10mg	3%	3%
Sodium 560mg	23%	30%
Total Carbohydrate 47g	16%	16%
Dietary Fiber 1g	4%	4%
Sugars 7g		
Protein 11g		
Vitamin A	0%	15%
Vitamin C	0%	0%
Calcium	10%	10%
Iron	15%	15%

* Amount in Box. When prepared with 2% lowfat milk, one serving (about 1 cup) contains an additional 14g total fat (3g sat. fat), 170mg sodium, and 1g total carbohydrate (1g sugars).

** Percent Daily Values are based on a 2,000 calorie diet. Your daily values may be higher or lower depending on your calorie needs:

	Calories:	2,000	2,500
Total Fat	Less than	65g	80g
Sat. Fat	Less than	20g	25g
Cholest	Less than	300mg	300mg
Sodium	Less than	2,400mg	2,400mg
Total Carb		300g	375g
Fiber		25g	30g

INGREDIENTS: ENRICHED MACARONI (ENRICHED FLOUR [FLOUR, NIACIN, FERROUS SULFATE, THIAMINE MONONITRATE, RIBOFLAVIN]); CHEESE SAUCE MIX (WHEY, DEHYDRATED CHEESE [GRANULAR AND CHEDDAR (MILK, CHEESE CULTURE, SALT, ENZYMES)], WHEY PROTEIN CONCENTRATE, SKIM MILK, CONTAINS LESS THAN 2% OF SALT, BUTTERMILK, SODIUM TRIPOLYPHOSPHATE, SODIUM PHOSPHATE, CITRIC ACID, YELLOW 5, YELLOW 6, LACTIC ACID)

CHUNK LIGHT TUNA IN WATER

Nutrition Facts

Serv. Size 2 oz. drained (56g / about ¼ cup)
Servings about 2.5
Calories 60
Fat Cal. 5

Amount/Serving	%DV*	Amount/Serving	%DV*
Total Fat 0.5g	1%	**Total Carb.** 0g	0%
Sat. Fat 0g	0%	Fiber 0g	0%
Cholest. 30mg	10%	Sugars 0g	
Sodium 250mg	10%	**Protein** 13g	23%

* Percent Daily Values (DV) are based on a 2,000 calorie diet. Vitamin A 0% • Vitamin C 0% • Calcium 0% • Iron 2% Niacin 20% • Vitamin B-6 8% • Vitamin B-12 20% • Phosphorus 8%

INGREDIENTS: LIGHT TUNA, WATER, VEGETABE BROTH, HYDROLYZED CASEIN, HYDROLYZED SOY PROTEIN, SALT.

1. Look up these
   words in a
   dictionary:
   *sodium
   phosphate,
   artificial citric
   acid, lactic
   acid, whey.*
2. Look up any
   other words
   from the labels
   you do not
   know. If one
   of the words
   is not in your
   dictionary, how
   could you find
   out what it
   means?
3. How would
   you define
   "processed"
   foods? How do
   processed foods
   differ from
   natural foods?
4. Which course in
   school would
   help people
   understand
   more about
   processed and
   natural foods?

Activity H Study the two food labels on page 84. Write the answers to the following questions on your paper.

1) What is the main ingredient in the macaroni?

2) What is the main ingredient in the cheese sauce mix?

3) What is the main ingredient in the can of tuna fish?

4) Which food has more calories per serving?

5) What does the abbreviation *DV* mean?

6) Which food has been enriched?

7) How many servings are in one can of tuna fish?

8) How many servings are in the macaroni and cheese?

9) Which food has the most protein?

10) Which food has the most fat?

11) What happens to the fat content when 2% milk is used to prepare the macaroni and cheese?

12) What percentage of the daily value of vitamin B-12 would you get from a serving of the tuna fish?

Part A Write out the meaning of each of these terms on your paper.

1) 18 g
2) 2 oz.
3) 1 pt.

4) 450°F
5) $\frac{1}{2}$ pkg.
6) 2 T.

7) $\frac{1}{2}$ tsp.
8) DV
9) one lb.

Part B On your paper, explain step-by-step what you would do to prepare the recipe below. Be sure to include a list of all the ingredients and utensils you will need.

Mexican Cole Slaw

Shred finely one head purple cabbage and three large peeled carrots into large bowl. Set aside. In a 2-cup screwtop jar combine:

2/3 c. olive oil
juice of one lemon or lime
2 tsp. ground black pepper
2 T. liquid hot sauce (optional)

1/3 c. water
2 tsp. onion powder
1 tsp. salt or to taste
1/4 c. brown sugar

Shake together in jar until well mixed. Pour liquid over cabbage and carrots. Toss well. Cover and set aside until serving time. Toss lightly before serving.

Part C Write the word or words on your paper that best complete each sentence.

1) To cook food quickly in a small amount of fat, _____ it.
   a) broil   b) sauté   c) simmer

2) A cook usually braises _____ .
   a) a T-bone steak   c) frozen vegetables
   b) meat that isn't tender

3) To *mince* an onion _____ .
   a) chop it up in small pieces   c) pull off the skin
   b) cook it until it is tender

Do It Yourself With How-To Books

How-to books

Reference books that provide detailed instructions for how to complete specific tasks.

How-to books tell you how to do something. You can probably find a how-to book to help you do anything you want to do. Some subjects of how-to books include:

All About Stamp Collecting	Be Your Own Lawyer
Introduction to the Guitar	How to Design and Sew Your Own Clothing
How to Make a Speech	
Pay Fewer Taxes—Legally!	Getting Started in Computing
Teach Yourself to Type	Improve Your Vocabulary
	Easy Home Repairs

Internet

The largest computer network in the world. It allows people from all over the world to use computers to interact with one another and to get information on a wide variety of topics.

Many how-to books are available on CD-ROM. You can also find how-to information on the **Internet**. The Internet is a large computer network. The Internet allows people from all over the world to use their computers to get information on a wide variety of topics. How-to information is also available on videocassettes that you can get at the library or a video store.

Activity A   Decide which of the following books probably tell you how to do something. Write their titles on your paper.

1) *Setting Up a Tropical Fish Tank*

2) *Do-It-Yourself Home Decorating*

3) *Building a Model Ship*

4) *The Red Pony*

5) *How to Care for Your Automobile*

6) *Two Dozen Wooden Toys to Make for Children*

7) *The History of the World*

8) *Complete Guide to Flower Gardening*

Following Directions

A how-to book provides step-by-step instructions that explain how to do or make something. Any materials that you will need to complete the task are listed. Photographs or drawings of the finished product are often shown.

A Birthday Calendar

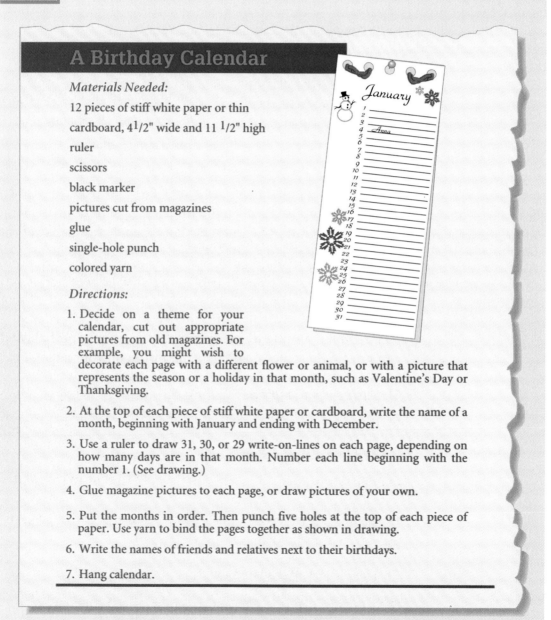

Materials Needed:

12 pieces of stiff white paper or thin cardboard, $4\frac{1}{2}$" wide and $11\frac{1}{2}$" high

ruler

scissors

black marker

pictures cut from magazines

glue

single-hole punch

colored yarn

Directions:

1. Decide on a theme for your calendar, cut out appropriate pictures from old magazines. For example, you might wish to decorate each page with a different flower or animal, or with a picture that represents the season or a holiday in that month, such as Valentine's Day or Thanksgiving.

2. At the top of each piece of stiff white paper or cardboard, write the name of a month, beginning with January and ending with December.

3. Use a ruler to draw 31, 30, or 29 write-on-lines on each page, depending on how many days are in that month. Number each line beginning with the number 1. (See drawing.)

4. Glue magazine pictures to each page, or draw pictures of your own.

5. Put the months in order. Then punch five holes at the top of each piece of paper. Use yarn to bind the pages together as shown in drawing.

6. Write the names of friends and relatives next to their birthdays.

7. Hang calendar.

USING WHAT YOU
HAVE LEARNED

Design and make
your own Birthday
Calendar. Follow
the directions on
page 88.

Activity B   Use the directions on page 88 to answer these questions. Write your answers on your paper.

1) What materials do you need to make the calendar?
2) What are the different tools that you will need?
3) What will you need the tools for?
4) How many pieces of paper do you need? Why?
5) Why should you decide on a theme before beginning?
6) What are the lines on each page for?
7) What is the purpose of the holes at the top of each page?

In some how-to books, the directions are written in paragraph form rather than listed step-by-step. The materials you will need to complete a project are included within the directions.

Activity C   Use these directions to answer the questions. Write your answers on your paper.

> **Setting Up an Aquarium**
> People have set up aquariums for thousands of years. The first aquarium would be as old as the ancient pyramids. In America, raising tropical fish is one of the most popular hobbies.
> You will need a fish tank, some lights, a heater and thermometer, a pump, and a filter. You will need some glass wool and charcoal for the filter. On the bottom, you will put some gravel. For cleaning the tank, get an algae scraper and a dip tube. A nylon fish net will be useful. Try some guppies for your first fish. They are very hardy.

1) What do the directions tell you how to do?
2) What materials will you need to buy or borrow to complete this project?
3) What instructions must you follow to complete this project? List the steps in order.

Activity D   List three things you would like to learn how to make or do. Take your list to the library and try to find at least one how-to book for each project.

Part A Read the paragraph below. Then write on your paper answers to the questions that follow.

Hanging a Mirror on a Door

If the door is very smooth, roughen it with sandpaper. Spread rubber cement on the back of the mirror. Put it about $\frac{1}{2}$ inch from the 4 edges. Press the mirror firmly on the door. Allow 24 hours for the cement to set.

---

1) What does the paragraph tell you how to do?

2) What materials will you need to complete this project?

3) What instructions must you follow to complete this project? List the steps in order.

Part B Follow the instructions below. Write your answers on your paper.

1) Think of a project you have done in the past.

2) Make a drawing of the completed project.

3) Write a list of the materials you used.

4) Write the directions you followed in order.

Magazine

A paperback publication with stories and articles on a variety of topics by different writers.

A **magazine** is a paperback publication. It has stories and articles by several writers. It usually has illustrations and advertisements. **Periodical** is another name for a magazine. A periodical comes out at regular **intervals**, such as daily, weekly, or monthly. An interval is a space of time between events. Some magazines are on CD-ROM. Some are also available through on-line computer services, including the Internet.

Kinds of Magazines

Periodical

A magazine published at regular intervals, such as daily, weekly, or monthly.

There are hundreds of different kinds of magazines to choose from. Most magazines have stories and articles for people with special interests.

Interval

The space of time between events.

News and Business	**Sports**
Time	Sports Illustrated
Newsweek	Sport
U.S. News and World Report	Golf Digest
Entertainment	World Tennis
TV Guide	Outdoor Life
Soap Opera Digest	Field and Stream
Rolling Stone	Triathlete
Stereo Review	**Hobbies and Special Interests**
People	Hot Rod
Magazines for Women	Apartment Life
Martha Stewart Living	Compute
Redbook	Computer User
Good Housekeeping	Byte
Ladies' Home Journal	PC Magazine
Magazines for Men	Scouting
Men's Health	Modern Photography
Men's Fitness	National Geographic
Men's Journal	Quilting Today
Men Talk	Astronomy

Digests

Digest

A magazine that contains summaries or condensed articles from other magazines.

Most people don't have time to read a lot of magazines. That is why digests are so popular. A **digest** is a periodical that has summaries of articles from other magazines. *Reader's Digest* is one of the most widely read magazines in the world. It was first published in 1922.

Condensed

A shorter version of an article but with the same main idea.

Many digests contain **condensed** articles from other publications. An article that is condensed is shortened but keeps the main ideas.

Below are some examples of popular digests. They have condensed articles from other publications, summaries of other publications, or very short original articles.

> **EXAMPLE**   *Golf Digest   Soap Opera Digest*
> *Book Digest   Reader's Digest*

Activity A   Follow the directions below. Write your answers on your paper.

1) Write a list of all the magazines that you have read or know about. Visit the library or a newsstand to refresh your memory.

2) Beside each title, write the general subject of the magazine. Use the bold subject heads on page 91 as a guide.

3) Put a circle around the magazines you subscribe to or read regularly.

4) Share your list with your class.

5) Bring old issues of magazines to class to share if possible.

Publication Cycles

Publish
To print and distribute magazines, books, newspapers, or other reading materials.

To **publish** means to print and distribute magazines, books, newspapers, or other materials. Most magazines are published monthly. A few magazines are published weekly. Some are published less often. This is referred to as the publication **cycle**. A cycle is the period of time needed for a certain event to repeat itself.

Cycle
The period of time between events, such as the publishing of a magazine.

Activity B   Match each numbered word on the left with its correct meaning on the right. Write each word and its meaning on your paper. Use a dictionary to help you.

1) daily   **a)** twice a month

2) weekly   **b)** twice a year

3) monthly   **c)** every day

4) annually   **d)** every other year

5) bimonthly   **e)** every other month

6) semimonthly   **f)** once a month

7) biannually   **g)** once a week

8) semiannually   **h)** once a year

Activity C   Write the answers to these questions on your paper. You may have to visit a library or newsstand to answer some of these questions.

1) Name a magazine that is published weekly.

2) Name a magazine that is published monthly.

3) What type of publication appears daily?

4) If a book is published once, is it a periodical?

5) Is an almanac a periodical? Explain why or why not.

6) Is an encyclopedia a periodical? Explain why or why not.

Subscription

A regular order for a magazine, newspaper, or other publication.

USING WHAT YOU HAVE LEARNED

Go to a library or a newsstand. Find an interesting magazine. Read it. Tell your class about the magazine. If possible, bring the magazine to class to show the others. Here are some questions to think about.

1. How much does it cost? How often is it published?

2. Who is this magazine for? Who would be interested in the articles?

3. How many pages does it have? How much of the magazine is advertising?

4. What are some of its special departments or regular features?

5. Would you recommend this magazine to others?

How to Get a Magazine

You can get a magazine in several ways:

- You can read one at the library.
- You can buy one at a newsstand.
- You can subscribe to one.

When you subscribe to a magazine, you fill out an order form to have the magazine sent to you by mail. You may enclose the payment for the **subscription** with the order form, or you may receive a bill later. The subscription rate is often lower than the newsstand rate.

Here is an example of a subscription order form.

Sports Car Digest

One-year subscription (12 issues):	$15.00
Two-year subscription (24 issues):	$27.00

SAVE 30% OVER THE NEWSSTAND RATE!

☐ Payment enclosed. ☑ Bill me later.

Name *Chris Williams*

Address *31 E. Ralston Place*

City/State/Zip *Wilton, Delaware   19999*

Signature *Chris Williams*

Activity D   Use the order form above to answer these questions. Write your answers on your paper.

1) How much does each issue of the *Sports Car Digest* cost with a one-year subscription?

2) How often is this magazine published?

3) Does the magazine cost less at the newsstand or by subscription?

4) Where might you get this magazine to read at no cost?

Finding Articles in Magazines

To learn what kinds of articles are in a magazine, look in the magazine's table of contents. The table of contents is usually near the front of the magazine. In some magazines, several pages of advertisements may come before the table of contents. In other magazines, the table of contents may appear on the cover as in the sample cover below.

Tropical Fish

The Hobbyist Magazine

Feature Articles

45 Choosing Your First Aquarium
49 Three Filter Systems You Should Think About
51 Raising Guppies
62 The Community Tank
by Joan Gillan

Columns

20 Fish Doctor *by Dr. H. Trye*
28 Fish of the Month *by Sammy Goldstein*

Departments

6 From the Editor's Desk
10 Letters to the Editor
69 Shopper's Guide

October, 1996
Vol. 5, No. 10

Activity E Use the sample magazine cover on page 95 to answer these questions. Write your answers on your paper.

1) What is the theme of this magazine?

2) Who is likely to read this magazine?

3) When was this issue of the magazine published?

4) How many feature articles are in this issue?

5) On what page do the letters to the editor begin?

6) If you had a one-year subscription to this magazine, how many more issues would you expect to get in 1996?

The Readers'
Guide to
Periodical
Literature

A magazine found in the library that lists articles from many other magazines.

You can use ***The Readers' Guide to Periodical Literature*** to find a specific magazine article. *The Readers' Guide* is a periodical. You can find it in the library. It lists articles from many magazines. The articles are listed by subject, title, and author. Here are some sample entries from *The Readers' Guide.*

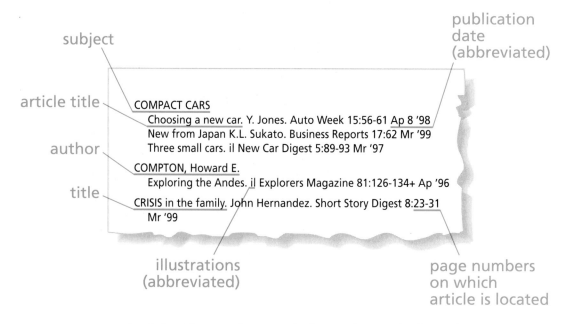

Labels on the image:
- subject
- publication date (abbreviated)
- article title
- author
- title
- illustrations (abbreviated)
- page numbers on which article is located

COMPACT CARS
  Choosing a new car. Y. Jones. Auto Week 15:56-61 Ap 8 '98
  New from Japan K.L. Sukato. Business Reports 17:62 Mr '99
  Three small cars. il New Car Digest 5:89-93 Mr '97
COMPTON, Howard E.
  Exploring the Andes. il Explorers Magazine 81:126-134+ Ap '96
CRISIS in the family. John Hernandez. Short Story Digest 8:23-31
  Mr '99

Activity F Use the sample from *The Readers' Guide* to answer these questions. Write your answers on your paper.

1) Which magazine is published weekly?

2) Which articles have pictures?

3) Who wrote the article "Crisis in the Family"?

4) Which magazine has an article by K. L. Sukato? What is the title of the article?

Lesson Review Write your answers to the following questions on your paper.

1) What is a periodical?

2) What are some different kinds of magazines? List at least three kinds and give one title for each kind. If necessary, look at the list on page 91.

3) Why might someone want to read a condensed version of an original article?

4) Give three examples of a publication cycle.

5) What is the most common interval for magazine publication?

6) Which magazine is published more often—a bimonthly or a semimonthly?

7) Which magazine is published more often—a semiannual or a biannual?

8) Where can you read magazines at no cost?

9) Which is usually less expensive—buying a magazine at a newsstand or having a subscription?

10) Is it possible that you would find an article from *Woman's Day* in *The Reader's Digest?*

11) Which magazine can help you locate an article— *The Reader's Digest* or *The Readers' Guide?*

Part A   Write the answers to the following questions on your paper.

1) What is the main information in a farmer's almanac?

2) Why would a mariner read a farmer's almanac?

3) Name one general information almanac.

4) Where is the index found in most almanacs?

5) Are you likely to find the answers to the following questions in an almanac—*Yes* or *No*?
   a) Has Denzel Washington ever won an Academy Award?
   b) How do you prepare Mexican Cole Slaw?
   c) Who holds the record for the most home runs?

Part B   Use this map to answer the questions below. Write your answers on your paper.

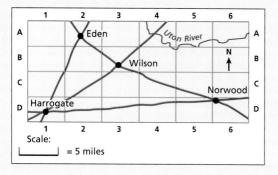

1) What two cities are southeast of Eden?

2) What city is located at D-1?

3) Is the Uton River north or south of Wilson?

4) What city is northwest of Wilson?

5) How many miles is it from Wilson to Norwood?

Part C   Write the answers to the following questions on your paper.

1) How are the articles in an encyclopedia arranged?

2) What is one book in a set of encyclopedias called?

3) What is a "desk" encyclopedia?

4) What would the guide letter be on volume one of *The World Book Encyclopedia*?

5) What would you expect to find at the top of each page of an encyclopedia?

Part D   Use the recipe below to answer the questions that follow. Write your answers on your paper.

Corn Pudding

1 17-oz. can creamed corn	1 small can evaporated milk
10 soda crackers, crushed	1 egg, beaten
salt	pepper

Grease a one-quart casserole dish. Pour in creamed corn. Add crushed soda crackers, evaporated milk, and egg. Add salt and pepper to taste. Mix well. Bake at 400°F until brown on top and bubbling (about 20-30 minutes).
Serves 4.

---

1) What steps should you follow to be sure the recipe turns out right?

2) What abbreviations are in this recipe and what do they mean?

3) What ingredients will you need to prepare this recipe?

4) What utensils will you need?

5) What directions must you follow to prepare this recipe? Write them in order.

Part E   Write the answer to these questions on your paper.

1) What kind of magazine has summaries of articles from other magazines?

2) Which magazine is published more often—a biannual or a semiannual?

3) Which of these reference books is a periodical—*The World Book Encyclopedia, Time Magazine, Betty Crocker's Picture Cookbook?*

4) What periodical helps you find articles in other periodicals?

5) Where can you look to learn what articles are in a magazine?

Test Taking Tip	When taking a true-false test, read each statement carefully. Write *true* only when the statement is true all of the time. Write *false* if any part or all of the statement is false.

The Telephone Book

Have you ever needed to find the phone number of a doctor or a dentist? Have you ever lost the phone number of a new friend? Whom do you call when a home appliance breaks down? The telephone book usually has the numbers you need. Knowing how to use the telephone book to find these numbers is a useful and an important skill.

In Chapter 4, you will learn about the sections of a telephone book. Most telephone books have at least two sections—the White Pages and the Yellow Pages. Some large telephone books have a third section—the Blue Pages. Each lesson is about a different section of the phone book and how to use that section.

Goals for Learning

▶ To recognize the different sections of a telephone book

▶ To learn to find numbers in the White Pages of the telephone directory

▶ To learn how to use the Yellow Pages to find information

▶ To learn to find numbers in the Blue Pages

A telephone book is also called a telephone directory. The **White Pages** are part of the telephone book. This part lists names, phone numbers, and addresses of the **residents** of an area. A resident is a person who lives in a certain place. The White Pages also list business and government agencies.

Residential Listings

Residential listings are arranged alphabetically by last name. To find a person's telephone number in the White Pages, you need to know his or her last name. Because people often have the same last name, it also helps to know a person's first name and address. When the last name is the same, the last name is sometimes printed only once.

White Pages

A part of the telephone book with residential, business, and government listings arranged in alphabetical order.

Resident

A person who lives in a certain place.

EXAMPLE

SANDERS Norma 1121 Millstream Dr Earton	**788-0990**
George F 1221 Haworth Av Earton	**788-9876**
Wm H 1288 Juniper Earton	**788-9980**
William & Wilma 2100 So Main Lawton	**889-2101**
SANTORO Kay 2111 Key St Earton	**788-5601**

More About Telephone Listings

- People's names are listed with the last name first. The name of the person who is responsible for paying the telephone bill is usually the person listed in the directory.
- More than one name may be listed for a single telephone. The publisher of the telephone book may charge a small **fee** to list additional names. A fee is a charge for a service.
- People may request an unlisted or unpublished telephone number. Their name and number do not appear in the telephone book. There is usually a fee for this service.

Fee

A charge for a service.

- The directory uses many abbreviations without punctuation.

EXAMPLES					
Jos	=	Joseph	Jr	=	Junior
Chas	=	Charles	Ret	=	Retired
Geo	=	George	&	=	and
St	=	Saint	MD	=	Medical Doctor

- The directory lists names the way people want them listed.

EXAMPLES	
Williams H Chas	Suarez Emelio & Anita E
Wing B W atty	Kostas Omar Mrs
Blackhorse John H	Sina G J MD

- A name that is listed with an initial comes before a first name that begins with the same letter.

EXAMPLES
Waters D
Waters David

- Some abbreviations are alphabetized as if they were spelled out. Notice that *St James* is alphabetized as if it were *Saint James.*

EXAMPLES
Sabato Isabella
St James Peter
Sanford Lance

- The telephone company usually publishes a new directory once a year. You may get a number that has not been published yet by calling Directory Assistance.

Activity A Write your answers to the following questions on your paper.

1) In what order would these names be listed in the telephone book—Raymond Mong, Charles Mendes, Maria Mulkern? Write the names as they would appear.

2) Which of these names would be listed first in the telephone book—Bonnie Hogan or B. Hogan?

3) Besides a person's last name, what are two other helpful things to know when you are looking up a person's number?

4) How would you get the telephone number of someone who has just moved to town?

5) How would you have your name listed in the telephone book? Give two different ways.

Business Listings

Businesses are sometimes listed in a special section of the White Pages and also in the **Yellow Pages**. In the White Pages, business names are listed alphabetically by the first word of the name of the business.

Yellow Pages

A part of the telephone book with business listings that are organized under subject headings arranged in alphabetical order.

EXAMPLES   Bob Wilsons Fine Foods

Jiffy Cleaners

More About Business Listings

• To find the telephone number of a business, you need the name of the business. It also helps to know the address.

• Businesses may ask to have their listing highlighted in bold, in extra-large letters, or some other way. There is usually a fee for this service.

• In business listings, the apostrophe (') may be left out. See the sample listing below for Jack Gillan's Electrical Service.

EXAMPLES   Jack Gillans Electrical Service

Jack Gillan Electrical Service

- Business names that are all capital letters, such as radio stations, are listed at the beginning of each letter section.

W

WNBD

W & W Dry Cleaners

Warner Insurance

- When *the* begins a business name, it usually follows the name. The name is alphabetized according to the first word after *the*.

Nazzaro Italian Grocery

Nelsons Kitchen Shop, The

Activity B   Write on your paper your answers to the following questions.

1) In which two sections of the directory could you look to find the number for Video Clips, a video store in your town?

2) Under what letter would you look to find the number for The Fancy Flounder Fish Market?

3) In what order would the business names below appear in the White Pages of the telephone book? Write the names as they would be printed.

WDMS-AM 1500

The Jacksons' Sport Center

WDMS-TV 5

George Jones Office Supplies

W & A Clothing

Jackson's Plumbing Supplies

Using Area Codes

Each part of the United States has its own area code. Your area code usually appears on the front of your directory. The directory also has a map that shows the area codes for each part of the United States. To call people who are not in your local calling area, you must dial their area code and then their telephone number. In most places, you must dial a 1 before the area code.

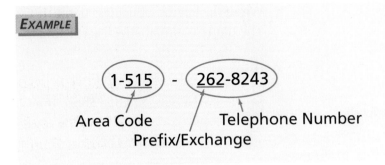

You may have to dial the area code to make some local calls. Check your directory to find out which local calls require an area code.

Activity C   Write on your paper your answer to these questions.

1) Which part of the following telephone number is the area code: 1-555-284-7890?

2) What is your area code? Write your telephone number with the area code.

3) How could you find out if you have to dial the area code to call towns or cities in your local calling area?

Directory Assistance

When you know someone's number, dial it directly. When you do not know the number, look for it in the directory. If the person or the business is not listed in your directory, you may call Directory Assistance. However, if a person has requested an unlisted number, Directory Assistance will not give out the number.

For local information, dial 411 for Directory Assistance. For long-distance information, dial: 1 + area code + 555-1212. If you do not know the area code, dial: 555-1212 or 1-555-1212. An operator will help you find the information you need. There is usually a charge for these services.

Toll-Free Numbers (800 Numbers)

> **Toll-free**
>
> *A long-distance number with an 800 area code.*

Many businesses have **toll-free** numbers. A toll-free number is a long-distance number with an 800 area code. Although the call is long distance, you do not have to pay for the call. The people you are calling pay for the call. To call an 800 number, dial 1-800 and then the number.

You may ask Directory Assistance for a toll-free number by dialing 1-800-555-1212.

International Calling

The telephone directory has directions for making international calls. It also lists calling codes for countries and cities around the world. You can dial foreign countries directly if you know the number.

EXAMPLES	International Access Code		Country Code		City Code	
London	011	+	44	+	1	+ Local Number
Cairo	011	+	20	+	2	+ Local Number

Activity D Use the information you've learned so far in this lesson. Answer each question. Write your answers on your paper.

1) What is the area code for toll-free numbers?

2) Where would you look in the directory to find the phone number for WSDE, a local radio station?

3) Which person would be listed first in the directory—D. L. Turner or Dwayne Turner?

4) What word would you look up to find the number for The Early Bird Cafe?

5) Fred Hernandez is new in town and not yet listed in the directory. How can you find out his number?

6) How can you find out the number for a business that is located in another state?

7) There are ten Robert Jacksons listed in the directory. What information will help you find the number for the Robert Jackson you wish to call?

8) What is another name for the telephone directory?

9) What is the area code in this telephone number: 1-345-564-6700?

10) What number would you call to get:

   a) local information?

   b) long-distance information?

   c) toll-free information?

Alternative Spellings for Names

Some names may be spelled in different, or **alternative**, ways. An alternative offers a choice between two or more possibilities. If you cannot find a name listed one way, think of another way the name may be spelled. Then look up the alternative spelling. Some directories provide cross-references for names with alternative spellings.

EXAMPLE

SCHWARZ ... *See Also Schwartz, Shwartz, Swartz*

Activity E Match the names in List 1 with their alternative spellings. Write each pair of names on your paper.

List 1	Alternative Spellings
1) Adkins	a) Louis
2) Smith	b) Miers
3) Jackman	c) More
4) Johnson	d) Atkins
5) Myers	e) Schaeffer
6) Michaelson	f) Bernsten
7) Johnston	g) Freedman
8) Bryan	h) Morgen
9) Berry	i) Allen
10) Bernstein	j) Johnstone
11) Thomas	k) Saunders
12) Stephens	l) Jackmon
13) Morgan	m) Brian
14) Moore	n) Tailor
15) Lewis	o) Stevens
16) Taylor	p) Barry
17) Allan	q) Jonson
18) Sanders	r) Smythe
19) Schaffer	s) Tomas
20) Friedman	t) Mickelson

Telephone Bills

Telephone companies charge fees for telephone services. Long distance calls cost more than local calls. Each long-distance call is **itemized**, or listed one by one, on a separate page of the bill. A bill is a request for payment of services. Here is a sample telephone bill.

```
A&T Tele-Com        CHARLES LEVINE              SEP 24,2001
                    ACCT (701)555-1234


    FROM LAST BILL

      $30.33 LAST BILL
     -30.33 PAYMENTS
         .00 THANK YOU FOR YOUR PAYMENT


    CURRENT CHARGES

      $25.76 LOCAL TELEPHONE CHARGES
        2.68 ITEMIZED CHARGES
        1.79 TAXES/MISC. CHARGES
      $30.23 TOTAL PAY BY OCT 24


        To Call the Business Office Dial (701) 555-3000
```

Activity F Use the sample telephone bill above to answer these questions. Write your answers on your paper.

1) What is Mr. Levine's telephone number?

2) What number should he call if he has questions about the charges on his bill?

3) How much does Mr. Levine owe for this month?

4) How much were the charges for long-distance calls?

Part A Use the information in the sample directory listings to answer the questions below. Write your answers on your paper.

VYSKOCIL Thomas A 58 Gale Pl Norwood.....**368-8900**	**WILMINGTON Grace** atty
Thomas J 4800 48th Pl Westport.................**456-8765**	54 Rand Ter Westport.................**456-9000**
	WINE A E MD
W	15 Durham St Suite 10 Southview.............**359-6000**
	Answering Service **359-5609**
WAAS Anne Jones Rt 1 Norwood.................**369-8700**	**Arnold Edward MD** 5601 56th Pl Westport....**456-6859**

1) What is the phone number of the attorney listed?

2) What is Dr. Wine's home phone number?

3) What number can you call if Dr. Wine is not at home or in his office?

4) How could you find out the area code for the towns listed in this directory?

5) What is the last name of Thomas J of 4800 48th Place?

WBQ TV REPAIR INC	
54 Rand Ter Westport.................**456-9005**	**WINE & CHEESE SHOP** 48 Sand Ln Norwood...**369-4000**
WEBB Broadcasting Station	**Wine Insurance Co**
5617 Webb Road Westport **457-5600**	34 Water Blvd Southview.................**359-7650**

6) Why is WEBB listed after WBQ TV Repair?

7) What has been left out of the name of the business located on Sand Lane in Norwood?

8) How could someone from out of the local area code find out if Wine Insurance Company has a toll-free number?

Part B Write the answer to these questions on your paper.

1) What are two reasons for calling Directory Assistance?

2) What calls are itemized on your monthly telephone bill?

Products and Services

Products

Goods that you can buy.

Services

What a business or individual can do for you.

The Yellow Pages is a classified telephone directory that lists businesses, **products**, and **services** for a city or town and its surrounding area. Products are goods that you can buy. A service is something that a business or individual does for you.

EXAMPLES	Products:	Automobiles, Carpet, Musical Instruments
	Services:	Automobile Repair, Carpet Installation, Music Lessons

Activity A Number your paper from 1 to 6. Beside each number, write whether the subject heading is a *product* or a *service*.

1) Travel Agents & Bureaus

2) Pianos—Tuning & Repair

3) Automobile Body Repairing

4) Pianos

5) Dolls—Retail

6) Moving & Storage

When you do not know the name of a business, use the Yellow Pages. To find a number in the Yellow Pages, you only need to know the type of business you are looking for.

You can also use the Yellow Pages to look up the telephone number of a specific business if you know its name.

The Yellow Pages also provides other useful information. In your Yellow Pages Directory you can find emergency numbers, an emergency medical guide, consumer information, local places of interest, a local ZIP code map, and a local road map.

Subject Listings

The classified listings in the Yellow Pages are arranged alphabetically by subject. Under each subject the individual businesses or professionals are also listed alphabetically.

EXAMPLE

Accountants

A E Smith Accounts 18 Wilton Ave Tanner ·········· 555-2093

ANDERSON DAVID E
Fredrick Bldg Rt 4 ······························· **555-0578**

ARNOLD JACK & SYLVIA

Professional accounts
Ready to serve you
6 days a week 9 to 5
45 W 25th St Sky City ·············· **555-6393**

Acupuncturists

ACUPUNCTURE REFERRAL SERVICE
205 Turnpike Road Cooksville ············· **800-555-8133**
Diaz Gloria 300 Main St ·························· 555-9111

Advertising Agencies

AdVantage Plus 29 E Balboa Rd ·························· 555-6983
ANNE RENOIR ADVERTISING
4229 Creve Coeur Ave Suite 23 ·············· **555-0443**
Creative Consultants
12289 W Third St ·························· 555-6191
Kandinsky / Rivera Assoc 615 Main St ·············· 555-2100

Activity B Use the sample Yellow Pages on page 113 to answer these questions. Write your answers on your paper.

1) What do A. E. Smith, David E. Anderson, and Jack and Sylvia Arnold have in common?

2) What information does the Arnolds' listing provide that the other two listings do not?

3) How would these three names be listed in the White Pages? Write them as they would appear.

4) Is there a long-distance charge for calling the Acupuncture Referral Service? How do you know?

5) Why might you call Gloria Diaz?

More About Subject Listings

Many subjects have several subtopics. These subtopics are also listed in alphabetical order. Notice that the following list of automobile topics are alphabetized by the word that follows *Automobile.*

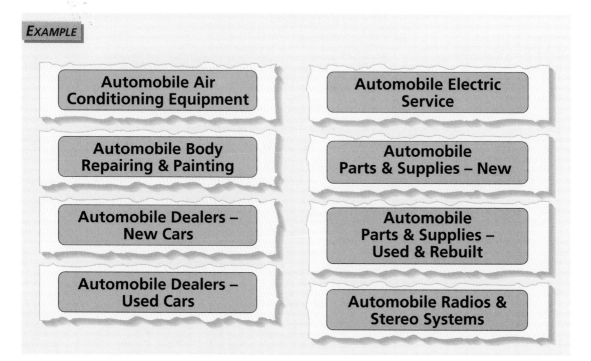

EXAMPLE

Automobile Air Conditioning Equipment

Automobile Electric Service

Automobile Body Repairing & Painting

Automobile Parts & Supplies – New

Automobile Dealers – New Cars

Automobile Parts & Supplies – Used & Rebuilt

Automobile Dealers – Used Cars

Automobile Radios & Stereo Systems

Activity C   Rewrite each list in alphabetical order on your paper.

List 1

Pianos
Pianos—Tuning & Repair
Piano & Organ Moving

List 2

Party Supplies—Renting
Party Planning Service
Party Supplies

List 3

Lawn Mowers
Lawn Maintenance
Lawn Mowers—Sharpening
    & Repairing

List 4

Dolls—Retail
Dolls—Repairing
Doll Houses & Accessories

Cross-References

Some subjects in the Yellow Pages have cross-references. See the example below.

EXAMPLE

♦ CAR DEALERS
See Automobile Dealers – New Cars
Also Automobile Dealers – Used Cars

Look in the index of this textbook to find out more about cross-references.

Professional Listings

A **profession** is a job, or occupation, that requires special information and often long academic training. A **professional** is someone who has a profession. Professionals provide a service to people.

EXAMPLES	Teacher	Attorney	Physician
	Architect	Accountant	Landscaper

Athletes and actors who receive pay for their work are also called professionals. The opposite of a professional athlete or actor is an amateur. An amateur is a person who does something for fun and is not paid.

Activity D   Write the answer to these questions on your paper.

1) What service does each of these professionals provide? Use a dictionary if necessary.

   teacher

   architect

   accountant

   attorney

   landscaper

   registered nurse

   pharmacist

   physician

   optometrist

2) What are three other professions? What service do they provide for others?

3) Maria plays on a baseball team for fun. Is she a professional or an amateur?

4) Why do you think a professional would pay to have his or her name listed in the Yellow Pages?

Advertisements in the Yellow Pages

Each business pays a fee to be listed in the Yellow Pages. The size of the fee depends on how the business wishes to be listed. Display ads and special listings cost more than regular listings. The size of the ad or listing also increases the fee. When a business chooses to have a display ad, the business name also appears in the regular listings.

EXAMPLE

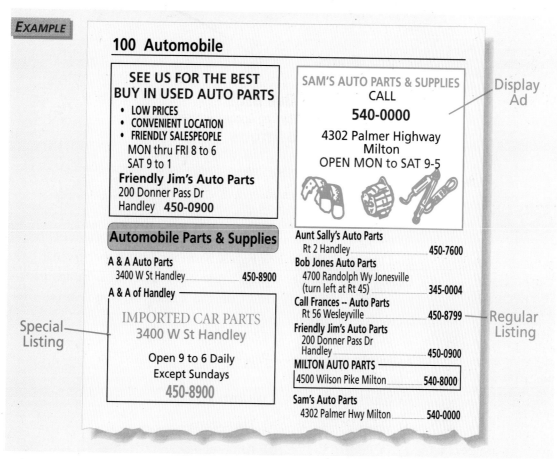

Activity E   Use the sample Yellow Pages listings above to answer these questions. Write your answers on your paper.

1) Which two companies have display ads and regular listings?

2) Which two companies have special listings?

3) Which businesses are open every day but Sunday?

4) Where is Bob Jones Auto Parts located?

5) What is the telephone number for A & A of Handley?

The Index of the Yellow Pages

The Yellow Pages directories for big cities are very large. Some come in two volumes. Subjects may be listed under several different topics. Many of these large directories provide an index. Using the index is often the quickest way to find the business you need.

EXAMPLE

Boots	**154**
Bowling	**156**
Bowling Ball Bags	
See Bowling Apparel & Accessories	**156**
Bows and Arrows	
See Archery Equipment & Supplies	**72**

Activity F   The following vocabulary exercise can help you find topics in the Yellow Pages. Number your paper from 1 to 9. Beside each number write a topic from Column 1. Beside each topic write the word from Column 2 that you might look up as a cross-reference for the topic.

Example   **1)** Dogs—Pets

Column 1	Column 2
1) Dogs	**a)** Physicians
2) Drinks	**b)** Apparel
3) Doctors	**c)** Boats
4) Attorneys	**d)** Beverages
5) Cars	**e)** Pets
6) Clothing	**f)** Chinaware
7) Film	**g)** Lawyers
8) Kayaks	**h)** Automobiles
9) Dishes	**i)** Motion picture

Part A   For which of the following situations would the Yellow Pages be most helpful? Choose only one item from each group. Write the letter of your choice on your paper.

1) **a)** You want to call Dr. Simon Vilas.

    b) You need the telephone number of the Franklin Drug Store.

    c) You want to call several stores to find out the price of a new television set.

2) **a)** You need the area code for Dallas, Texas.

    b) You need the ZIP code for a town in your state.

    c) You want to call the Handley Movie Theater to find out when the next show begins.

3) **a)** You have a question about your phone bill.

    b) You need to call a dentist.

    c) You lost your best friend's phone number.

4) **a)** You want to find a school that teaches computer science.

    b) You want the number of your high school.

    c) You need to call your aunt Rebecca.

Part B   Write the answer to these questions on your paper.

1) How are listings in the Yellow Pages different from those in the White Pages?

2) How are listings organized in the Yellow Pages?

3) Will you find residential listings in the Yellow Pages?

4) What is one product and one service that might be listed in the Yellow Pages?

5) What are two kinds of professionals who might be listed in the Yellow Pages?

Blue Pages

A part of the telephone book that lists the numbers of government agencies.

Some telephone books have a separate section called the **Blue Pages** that lists government agencies. The Blue Pages lists numbers for the city, county, state, and federal governments.

EXAMPLE

GOVERNMENT OFFICES

GOVERNMENT – CITY

GALESVILLE - CITY OF –

City Clerk's Office	255-7942
Economic Development	255-6000
Fire Dept	
Emergency calls Dial 9-1-1	
or	255-9865
Mayor's Office	255-8740
Police Dept	255-4000
Crime Solvers	255-4002
Drug Hot Line	255-4001
Emergency calls Dial 9-1-1	
Public Information	255-6859

GOVERNMENT – COUNTY

GALES - COUNTY OF –

Aging, Department of	222-2222
Toll Free	800-555-2222
Finance Department	222-9810
Property Tax	222-1000
Water & Sewer	222-1001
Information	222-5000
Sheriff	
Civil Court Process	222-3000
Warrant	222-4000
Circuit Court	222-1600
Domestic Relations	222-9000

GOVERNMENT – STATE

Attorney General	800-772-9801
Dept of Motor Vehicles	800-772-9900

GOVERNMENT – FEDERAL

Environmental Protection Agency	202-562-2090
Internal Revenue Service	202-829-1040
Social Security Administration	
Toll Free	800-772-1213
Hearing Impaired—TDD Only	
Toll Free	800-325-0778
Veterans Administration	800-827-1000

The Blue Pages of the telephone book may be on blue paper, or they may have a blue outer edge.

USING WHAT YOU HAVE LEARNED

Look in the Blue Pages in your telephone directory. Find these numbers.

a) Your sheriff

b) The department of motor vehicles

c) The library

Activity A   Use the sample Blue Pages above to answer these questions. Write your answers on your paper.

1) What number would you use to contact the Social Security Administration if you were hearing impaired? Is there a charge for this call?

2) Is the Attorney General a city, state, or federal official? What is the Attorney General's number?

3) What number would a person in Gales County call with questions about his or her property tax?

4) What number should a person in Galesville call with information about a crime?

Part A   On your paper, write the section or sections of the telephone book you would look in to find the telephone numbers for each of the following. Write on your paper *WP* for White Pages, *YP* for Yellow Pages, or *BP* for Blue Pages.

Examples   Michelle DeFalco—**WP**   a dentist—**YP**
              Whitehorse Art Studios—**WP, YP**   the sheriff—**BP**

1) The fire department

2) A piano tuner

3) John's Auto Repair

4) Roberto Martinez

5) An attorney

6) The Social Security Administration

7) Rosa's Pizza

8) Derek C. Jones

9) Department of Aging

10) A lawn mower repairer

Part B   Write on your paper the answer to these questions about the Blue Pages.

1) What are the four levels of government agencies usually listed in the Blue Pages?

2) What type of agency is the Social Security Administration?

3) How are the agencies listed under each level of government?

Part A Use the facts in the sample directory page below to answer the following questions. Write your answers in complete sentences on your paper.

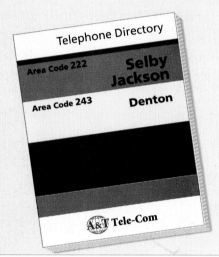

D'ZMURA T 15 Eaton Ln Denton 450-4321	EDGE Wm C 80 W St Jackson............................ 349-0837
DZWONCHYK Martha Rt 4 Selby...................... 343-7654	EDGERION John & Susan 24 Tulip Dr Denton... 450-3410
E	EDISON M K MD 3 Howard Plaza Selby 342-5400
EJ's Pizza Rt 4 Selby................................... 343-8700	If no answer call 342-1740
E Smith Inc 601 Rouse Way Jackson 349-0837	EDISON Inc. contractors
EDDY R Frank 39 Wither Av Denton 450-0426	140 Town Hwy Jackson 349-9090
	EDWARDS C Attorney 4 Howard Plaza Selby 342-4000

1) What towns does this directory cover?

2) What is Bill Edge's telephone number?

3) What is M. K. Edison's profession? How can you tell?

4) Would Frank Eddy have to use an area code to order a pizza from EJ's? Write the number as he would have to dial it.

5) Which of the listings on this page would probably also be found in the Yellow Pages?

Part B   From each pair of situations that follow, choose the one in which the person would be most likely to use the Yellow Pages. Write the letter of your choice on your paper.

1) a) Elena Wong needs a plumber. Her sister Dolores recommends John J. Rowlands, Inc.

   b) John Williams has a toothache. He needs to call a dentist.

2) a) Maria Sanchez needs to call the Walton Library.

   b) Nancy Gillan wonders where she can buy computer supplies.

3) a) Margaret wants to find an Italian restaurant near her office.

   b) Mr. Wilson needs to call Erlickson Dry Cleaning Company.

4) a) Robert forgot his friend Lamar's phone number.

   b) Chris needs to find a company that sells nursing uniforms.

5) a) Mrs. Simone wants to buy five large pizza pans.

   b) Doris Williams wants to call Wilson Department Store.

Part C   Write answers to the following questions.

1) What is listed in the White Pages? the Yellow Pages?

2) What kinds of listings are in the Blue Pages?

3) Would you find a number for the School Department in the Blue Pages? Why or why not?

4) In which section of the directory would you look to find the telephone numbers for City Hall? for an auto supply store?

5) These federal agencies are listed in the Blue Pages: Interior, Department of; Medicare; Consumer Products Safety Commission. Write the listings in the order in which they appear.

| Test Taking Tip | When taking a multiple-choice test, cross out any answers that you know for sure are incorrect. From the remaining answers, choose the one that seems most correct. |

Chapter 5

Using a Library to Find Information

The library is the best place to look for information. Nowhere else is so much information on so many different subjects in one place. At first glance, you may think that the library is too big and has too much information. How will you ever find what you are looking for? All libraries, big and small, follow a similar plan for arranging books and other resources. You can understand that plan. It will help you find the information you are looking for.

In Chapter 5, you will learn about libraries. You will understand the kinds of resources libraries have. You will learn how those resources are organized. You will learn how to find the information you need.

Goals for Learning

▶ To learn how to find information in a library

▶ To learn about the types of materials available in a library

▶ To learn to recognize and find fiction materials

▶ To learn how to find nonfiction books using the Dewey Decimal System

When people think about libraries, they usually think about books. Today, however, libraries are about more than books. Today, libraries have a wide variety of print materials as well as audiovisual materials and equipment. Because of this, some libraries today are called media centers.

Print Materials in a Library

Here are some of the print materials you will find in most libraries.

Hardback books	Books in hardcover include fiction and nonfiction. You can check out most of these books.
Paperback books	Most libraries have collections of paperback, or softcover, books that can be checked out.
Reference books	The reference section has encyclopedias, atlases, and other books. You usually cannot check out books in the reference section. You must use these books in the library.
Magazines	Libraries subscribe to many kinds of magazines. The most recent issues are usually displayed on a rack. Old issues are kept on separate shelves. You often have to ask the librarian to get them for you.
Newspapers	Most libraries subscribe to all the local newspapers. Some get newspapers from other cities. The library keeps old issues on file. Ask your librarian for help.
Telephone books	You can find local telephone books in your library. Some libraries have copies of telephone books from other cities.
Guides	Libraries have many kinds of guides and handbooks. You can look in guides to colleges and vocational schools to find out about their programs and requirements.

Activity A What kind of print material would you look for in the library for each situation? Write your answers on your paper.

1) You are moving to a new city and plan to rent an apartment. You need the number of a service in that city to help you.

2) You plan to go to the community college in the fall and want to know if it offers courses in electronics.

3) You want to read an article in last February's *The Reader's Digest.*

4) You want to find a part-time job.

5) You want to look at a map of Chile.

Audiovisual Materials in a Library

Here are some of the audiovisual materials you will find in most libraries.

Videotapes	Videotape cassettes store motion pictures on tape. These may be movies, nonfiction documentaries, training programs, or other productions. Videotapes are often stored on the shelves alongside books. Videotapes are played on VCRs.
Compact discs (CDs)	CDs store music. Computer information is stored on CD-ROMs. (ROM stands for "Read Only Memory.") One CD-ROM can hold an entire encyclopedia with color photographs, video, sound, and text. You need a CD player to play music CDs. You need a computer with a CD-ROM drive to access information on a CD-ROM.
Videodiscs	A videodisc is similar to a CD. Videodiscs can store print and motion pictures. Some libraries have movies and encyclopedias stored on videodisc. You need a videodisc player and a television or a computer monitor to view the information on a videodisc.
Other materials	Libraries may also have other items that you can check out or use in the library. These may include copy machines, personal computers and software, videocassette recorders, videodisc players, televisions, filmstrips, audiocassettes, and records. Ask the librarian for available resources.

Other Libraries

To borrow books from a public library, you usually need a library card. In some cities and towns, you must be a resident to get a library card. In other places, you must only be a resident of the state. You can get a library card by filling out a simple application. You may be asked for a Social Security number, your driver's license, or some other form of identification. If you do not have one of these, you may need an adult who already has a card to sponsor you.

In most places, the city or county government operates the local public library. Depending on where you live, your county library may have one branch or many branches. A **branch** is one of the libraries in a system. If your library is part of a system, you can use your card to borrow books and other materials from any of the branches in the system.

USING WHAT YOU HAVE LEARNED

Make a list of the equipment and materials that you read about in this lesson. Go to your school library or your public library. Find out what is available in your area. The next time you want information, don't overlook these resources.

Students find libraries useful for doing research and studying for classes.

Finding Material in a Library

Libraries have thousands and sometimes millions of different books and other materials. To make these materials easy to find, libraries list them in **catalogs.** Here are some kinds of catalogs in a library.

Library catalog	A **library catalog** lists most of the materials in a library. It may be printed on index cards or stored on a computer or on **microfiche.** The materials may include fiction and nonfiction books, videotapes, and other types of materials. There are three types of listings: title, author, and subject. Newspapers are not usually included in the main library catalog.
Magazine catalog	A **magazine catalog** lists all the magazines a library subscribes to. It identifies the issues the library has.
Newspapers	A library has a list of the newspapers it subscribes to and all of the old issues it has. The old issues of some newspapers may be stored on microfilm or microfiche.
Video catalog	A **video catalog** lists all the films and videotapes a library owns by title or subject.

Activity B For each item, decide which catalog each person should look at. Write your answers on your paper.

1) Ramon wants to find a nonfiction book about volcanoes.
2) Chan wants to know if the library has a copy of the December 1994 issue of *Personal Computing.*
3) Mary wants to know if the library has the movie *Dances With Wolves.*
4) Mr. Jackson wants to know if the library has any books of Jack London's short stories.
5) Chris would like to read an article in the sports section of the September 25, 1995, issue of *Fieldstone Daily News.*

The Library of Congress

Library of Congress

The national library of the United States.

The **Library of Congress** is in Washington, D.C. It serves as the national library of the United States. Congress started the library in 1800 for its members. Now the Library of Congress also serves other government agencies, scholars, other libraries, and the general public.

In 1815, Congress bought Thomas Jefferson's library, which had 6,000 volumes. Today, the library has over 80 million items in 470 languages. The library has books, pamphlets, periodicals, films, videocassettes, CDs, photographs, music, and maps.

For more information about our national library, write:

Library of Congress
101 Independence Avenue SE
Washington, DC 20540

Activity C   Answer on your paper these questions about the Library of Congress.

1) Where is the Library of Congress?
2) Who owned the original 6,000 volumes in the Library of Congress?
3) About how many items does the Library of Congress own today?
4) Besides books, what are three other kinds of materials found in the Library of Congress?
5) Who can use the Library of Congress?

Part A   Write the answers to these items on your paper.

1) Because of the kinds of materials they have, what are libraries sometimes called today?

2) Name at least two types of print materials other than books that you would find in most libraries.

3) Name two types of audiovisual materials that many libraries have today.

4) Name two other kinds of equipment that you might find in a library.

5) What is the name for lists of materials in libraries?

Part B   For each of the following items, decide what kind of material each person should look for at the library. Write your answers on your paper.

1) Ruby wants the telephone number of an organization in another city.

2) Ben wants to use an encyclopedia on computer.

3) Elena would like to watch the movie *Forrest Gump*.

4) Ossie needs extra help learning Spanish. It would help if he could hear the correct pronunciation of words.

5) Kimi wants to know the entrance requirements at the local community college.

6) Richard is interested in finding out about a major earthquake that occurred a year ago.

Autobiography
A story of a real person's life written by that person.

Biographical novel
A fictional account of a real person's life.

Biography
A nonfiction book about a real person written by someone other than that person.

Dialogue
Conversation.

Fiction
An imaginary story.

Historical novel
A fictional story about real people and events.

History
A nonfiction book about real people and events of the past.

Nonfiction
Based on facts.

Novel
A long, complex story.

Short story
A story that can usually be read in one sitting.

Fiction is an imaginary story. **Nonfiction** is based on facts.

Novels and short stories are two kinds of fiction. A **novel** is a long story with many characters and events. Usually, the story has several twists and turns before the final outcome. Most novels are several hundred pages long. Some, such as *Gone With the Wind* by Margaret Mitchell, may be more than 1,000 pages. Others, such as *The Red Pony* by John Steinbeck, have fewer than 100 pages. Short novels are sometimes called novellas.

A **short story** may be only one or two pages long. It may also be as long as several dozen pages. Many short stories are first printed in magazines. You may also find collections of short stories in a book. Literature textbooks often have short stories.

Most fiction is about imaginary people and events. Sometimes, however, authors include real people and events in their stories. They might use actual words that the people said. Sometimes authors make up words for people to say. Authors also combine facts and imagination to write about the way events may have happened.

Here are five kinds of fiction and nonfiction books.

Biography	A book about a real person written by someone else. All of the events actually happened. If there is **dialogue,** or conversation, it is the exact words that someone said.
Autobiography	A story about a real person written by that person. If you write a story about your own life, it is an autobiography.
Biographical novel	A story about a real person. The author adds imaginary dialogue and imaginary events.
History	A nonfiction book about real people and events of the past.
Historical novel	A story about real people and events. The author adds imaginary dialogue and events.

If you are not sure whether a book is fiction or nonfiction:

- Look for the word *novel* or *short story* on the cover or title page.
- Check to see if the book is marked with an *F* or *FIC* for fiction. If it is, it is stored in the fiction section of the library.

Activity A   Make two columns on your paper. Write *Fiction* at the top of one column and *Nonfiction* at the top of the other. Look over the five kinds of books described on page 132. List them in the correct columns. Beside each type of book, write a title of a real book that is an example of that type. You may need to go to your school library to complete this activity.

How Fiction Books Are Arranged in the Library

All libraries arrange fiction books in alphabetical order according to the authors' last names. Some authors have written many books. Their books will be grouped together and arranged in alphabetical order by title. The words *the, a,* or *an* are not used to alphabetize titles.

EXAMPLE   These books by John Steinbeck would be arranged in the following order:
    Cannery Row
    The Grapes of Wrath
    Of Mice and Men
    The Red Pony

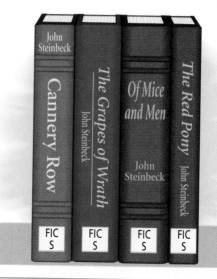

If two authors share the same last name, the books are arranged in alphabetical order according to the authors' first names.

> **EXAMPLE** *The Count of Monte Cristo* by Alexandre Dumas
> *Jonoah and the Green Stone* by Henry Dumas

USING WHAT YOU HAVE LEARNED

Look in your Sunday newspaper this week. Find out what the best-sellers are in hardcover and paperback fiction and nonfiction.

Make a list of the topics that people like to read about. Here are some examples.

Fiction:
    Spy stories
    Romance

Nonfiction:
    Biographies
    How to make
      money

Some libraries group certain types of fiction books together. For example, they might put all the mystery books in one section. They might put all the science fiction books in another section. As with other fiction books, these books will be arranged in alphabetical order. The order will be according to the authors' last names within that section.

Activity B   Arrange these fiction books in the order that they would appear on a shelf in a library. Write the books in order on your paper.

1) *The Outsiders* by S. E. Hinton

2) *White Fang* by Jack London

3) *Hawaii* by James Michener

4) *That Was Then, This Is Now* by S. E. Hinton

5) *Seventeenth Summer* by Maureen Daly

6) *Call of the Wild* by Jack London

7) *Huckleberry Finn* by Mark Twain

8) *Wuthering Heights* by Emily Brontë

9) *Jane Eyre* by Charlotte Brontë

10) *Treasure Island* by Robert Louis Stevenson

11) *Watership Down* by Richard Adams

12) *Superfudge* by Judy Blume

13) *The Wrestling Match* by Buchi Emecheta

14) *Dragonsong* by Anne McCaffrey

15) *Kidnapped* by Robert Louis Stevenson

Finding a Fiction Book in a Library

Finding a fiction book in the library can be easy if you remember the following guidelines:

- To find a fiction book on the library shelf, you need to know the author's last name and the title of the book.

- To find a fiction book when you know the title but not the author's name, use the library catalog. The library catalog has records for each book. Each book has an author record and a title record. Some fiction books have subject records. If you look up the title or the subject of the book, you will find the author's name.

- If you search for a book on a computer catalog, you can type the author's name, the title, or the subject. The computer catalog will list all of the books that were written by that author. It will also list the books that have that title or are about that subject.

Activity C Decide if you would look up the title record, author record, or subject record for each item in the library catalog. Write on your paper *A* for author, *T* for title, or *S* for subject.

1) *Gone With the Wind*

2) Margaret Mitchell

3) the Civil War

4) *Huckleberry Finn*

5) Mark Twain

6) adventure and adventurers

7) sailing

8) *Moby Dick*

9) Herman Melville

10) ocean travel

Part A ␣ Write the answers to the following questions on your paper.

1) Here are some famous fiction stories. Are they novels or short stories?

   a) "The Tell-Tale Heart" by Edgar Allan Poe. (9 pages)

   b) *20,000 Leagues Under the Sea* by Jules Verne. (447 pages)

   c) "The Most Dangerous Game" by Richard Connell. (13 pages)

2) Write the following book titles in the order that they would appear on a shelf in the fiction section of the library.

   The Kitchen God's Wife by Amy Tan
   The Grapes of Wrath by John Steinbeck
   The Joy Luck Club by Amy Tan
   Ceremony by Leslie Marmon Silko

3) What are two ways that you can recognize a fiction book in a library?

4) What do you need to know to find a fiction book on a library shelf?

Part B ␣ Match each type of book with its description. Write the item number and the matching letter on your paper.

1) Historical novel   **a)** A book about someone's life written by that person

2) History   **b)** A book about a real person written by someone else

3) Biography   **c)** A fictional story about a real person

4) Biographical novel   **d)** A book about real people and events of the past

5) Autobiography   **e)** A fictional story about real people and events of the past

What is a nonfiction book?

A nonfiction book is about real people, real events, facts, or people's ideas.

How can I recognize a nonfiction book?

Bibliography

A list of books and articles an author has used as references to write a book. Bibliographies usually appear in the back of the book.

Nonfiction books often have a reference list or **bibliography.** These are the books and articles the author consulted when writing the book. Look for the references in the back of the book.

Nonfiction books often have indexes. An index is an alphabetical list of the topics included in the book. Look at the index at the end of this book.

In a library, a nonfiction book has a number on the binding. Under the number are the first one or two letters of the author's last name.

Who was Dewey?

Dewey Decimal System

A system that libraries use to classify and organize books.

Melvil Dewey was a librarian who lived from 1851 to 1931. In 1876, he invented a system for arranging books in a library. Today, this system is called the **Dewey Decimal System.** Dewey also started the first school for training librarians. He taught his system to his students.

What is a decimal system?

Call number

The numbers and letters assigned to a library book. The call number determines where the book will be placed on the shelf.

Decimals are based on the number ten. Dewey divided the information in nonfiction books into ten main subject areas. He used the numbers from 000 to 999 to cover the fields of general knowledge. He used decimals and letters to fit special subjects within each group. The **call number** on the spine of a book shows these numbers and letters.

Each book has three numbers before the decimal point. It may have several numbers after the decimal point. Several books with the same number are alphabetized by author's last name.

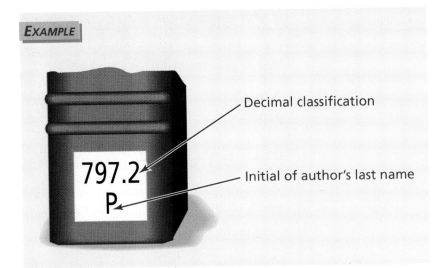

Decimal classification

797.2
P

Initial of author's last name

How can the Dewey Decimal System help me?

To find a book in the library catalog, you use one of these three things:

- the title

- the author's name

- the subject

The record in the catalog gives the Dewey Decimal numbers, or call number. Suppose a book has the call number 797.2/P. First find the 700 shelves in the nonfiction section of the library. Skim the shelves, looking for the 790s. Then find the books with 797.2. Finally, look for the books with the letter *P*.

What if the book I want isn't there?

All of the books with the same number are about the same subject. If you know the number that matches your subject, you can find other books on that subject.

Do I need to memorize the whole Dewey Decimal System?

Since the call numbers are on the catalog records, it is not necessary to memorize the numbers. However, it is helpful to know the system's ten main groups.

What are the ten main categories of the Dewey Decimal System?

Numbers	Subjects and Subtopics
000–099	General Works *Encyclopedias, periodicals, library facts*
100–199	Philosophy and Psychology *Logic, mental health*
200–299	Religion *Mythology*
300–399	Social Sciences *Government, education, economics*
400–499	Language *Dictionaries, foreign languages, grammar*
500–599	Pure Sciences *Biology, mathematics, botany, chemistry*
600–699	Technology (Applied Sciences) *Engineering, aviation, home economics*
700–799	Arts and Recreation *Fine art, music, sports, architecture*
800–899	Literature *Poetry, plays, speeches, humor*
900–999	History and Geography *Travel, biography*

How are main topics divided?

Each main topic is divided into subtopics.

EXAMPLE

History and Geography	900–999	900–909	General History
		910–919	Travel
		920–929	Biography and Autobiography

How are nonfiction books arranged on the shelf?

Nonfiction books are arranged by number first. Then they are put in order by the author's last name. Study these examples closely:

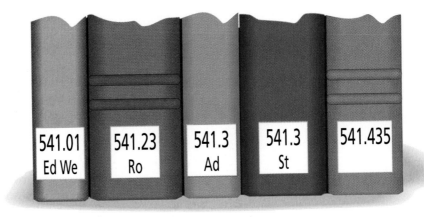

Are there any exceptions to the Dewey Decimal System that I should know about?

The purpose of the system is to help people find books. With biographies, you are more interested in the subject than in the author. Biographies are arranged alphabetically according to the person whom the book is about. For example, *My Life* by Golda Meir, an autobiography, would come before *Adlai Stevenson of Illinois* by John Bartlow Martin. Alphabetically, *Meir* comes before *Stevenson*.

Activity A   Write the main topic heading and numbers of the Dewey Decimal System for each type of book listed below. Write your answers on your paper.

1) Greek mythology

2) Computer science

3) Southwest region

4) Poetry

5) Sports

6) Mental health care

7) Library science

8) English grammar

9) Advanced math

10) Education in the United States

Activity B Use the facts on pages 137–140 to answer these questions. Write your answers on your paper.

1) You see the number 920 on a book. What subject is it about?

   a) Travel

   b) Geography

   c) Biography

2) You want to read *The Babe Ruth Story* by Howard Smith. Should you look for *Smith* or *Ruth* alphabetically on the shelf?

3) Who invented the system that most libraries use to arrange books?

   a) Melvil Dewey

   b) Thomas Jefferson

4) Will you find the letter *N* or a call number on nonfiction books at the library?

5) You need to know at least one of three things to find a nonfiction book in the library catalog. What are these three things?

6) In which category would you expect to find an encyclopedia?

   a) Pure Sciences

   b) General Works

   c) History

7) Which of these books would come first on the shelf?

USING WHAT YOU HAVE LEARNED

- Write down five subjects that you would like to know more about.
- Take your list to the library.
- Look up your subjects in the library catalog.
- Write down the complete Dewey Decimal number for a book on that subject.
- Find that book on the library shelves.

**The Dewey Decimal System
- Main Headings -**

000–099	General Works
100–199	Philosophy and Psychology
200–299	Religion
300–399	Social Sciences
400–499	Language
500–599	Pure Sciences
600–699	Applied Sciences
700–799	Arts and Recreation
800–899	Literature
900–999	History and Geography

Lesson Review Write the main heading and numbers that would be used to classify a book on each of the subjects listed below. Use the information above and on page 139. Write your answers on your paper.

Example A book about modern art—**Arts and Recreation, 700s**

1) A math book
2) A poetry book
3) Shakespeare's plays
4) A Bible
5) Psychology
6) An atlas
7) A book about the Dewey Decimal System
8) A cookbook
9) How to build a ship
10) Famous paintings
11) Football rules
12) How to build a computer
13) Traveling in Europe
14) O. Henry's short stories
15) Life story of Hank Aaron
16) Growing vegetables
17) A geometry book
18) *Life Skills English*
19) World Almanac
20) A dictionary

Finding information in a library can be easy as long as you follow some simple guidelines. At times you may follow these guidelines and still cannot find what you need. If this happens, do not hesitate to ask a librarian for help.

How to Find What You Need

Here's how to find a book in the library using either the computer or the card catalog.

Step 1	Find the entry for the book you want. Use either the title record, author record, or subject record.
Step 2	Copy the complete call number for nonfiction books on a piece of paper. For a fiction book, you only need the author's name and title.
Step 3	Find the section of the library that has the book you want. If you are not familiar with the library layout, check with the librarian. Many libraries post a map of the library layout near the checkout desk.
Step 4	Use the call number to find the book on the shelf.

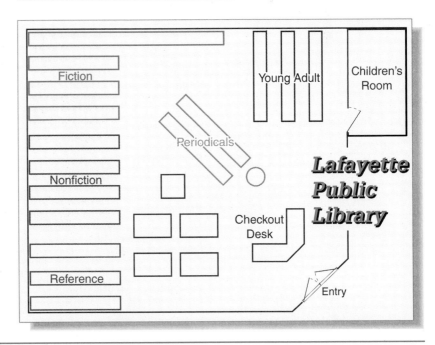

Understanding Call Numbers

The Dewey Decimal number appears on the back of each nonfiction book. You may see other letters before the number:

R = Reference Y or YA = Young Adult J = Juvenile

An F or FIC sometimes labels fiction books. A special label may also appear:

M = Mystery SS = Short Story Collection
R = Romance SF = Science Fiction

Records in the Library Catalog

Most libraries have switched from card catalog drawers to a computer catalog. Some smaller libraries and school libraries may still use a card catalog. The three kinds of cards in a card catalog are author card, title card, and subject card. Each card has the same facts arranged differently.

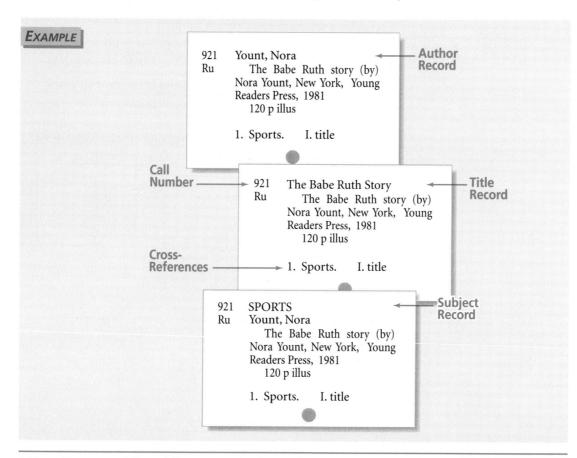

EXAMPLE

921 Yount, Nora
Ru   The Babe Ruth story (by)
Nora Yount, New York, Young
Readers Press, 1981
120 p illus

1. Sports.   I. title

← Author Record

Call Number →

921 The Babe Ruth Story
Ru   The Babe Ruth story (by)
Nora Yount, New York, Young
Readers Press, 1981
120 p illus

← Title Record

Cross-References →

1. Sports.   I. title

921 SPORTS
Ru   Yount, Nora
The Babe Ruth story (by)
Nora Yount, New York, Young
Readers Press, 1981
120 p illus

1. Sports.   I. title

← Subject Record

Activity A Use the information on the cards on page 144 to answer these questions. Write your answers on your paper.

1) What is the complete title of the book?

2) Who is the author of the book?

3) Is this book a biography or an autobiography?

4) What is the complete call number?

Other Facts in a Record

The record also provides other useful information about a book, including:

- the place the book was published.

- the publisher's name.

- the copyright date, or what year the book was published. This tells you how current the information and facts in the book are.

- the number of pages in the book.

- whether the book is illustrated.

Activity B Use the information on the cards on page 144 to answer these questions. Write your answers on your paper.

1) Where and when was this book published?

2) Who is the publisher?

3) How many pages does the book have?

4) Does this book have pictures?

Edit

To get written material ready for publication.

You may also see the notation *ed* before or after a person's name in a record. This means that the person has edited the book. To **edit** means to prepare written material for publication.

Using a Computer Catalog

Most libraries today keep their records on a computer.

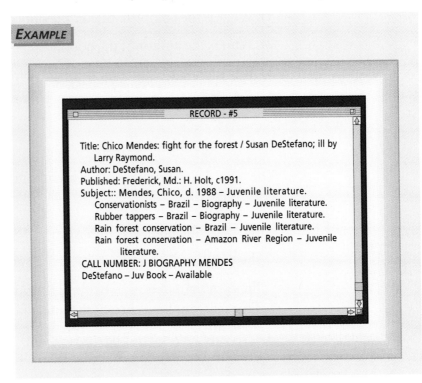

EXAMPLE

RECORD - #5

Title: Chico Mendes: fight for the forest / Susan DeStefano; ill by
    Larry Raymond.
Author: DeStefano, Susan.
Published: Frederick, Md.: H. Holt, c1991.
Subject:: Mendes, Chico, d. 1988 – Juvenile literature.
    Conservationists – Brazil – Biography – Juvenile literature.
    Rubber tappers – Brazil – Biography – Juvenile literature.
    Rain forest conservation – Brazil – Juvenile literature.
    Rain forest conservation – Amazon River Region – Juvenile
      literature.
CALL NUMBER: J BIOGRAPHY MENDES
DeStefano – Juv Book – Available

To find a book using a computer catalog, follow the instructions on the screen.

Step 1	Enter the title, author, or subject of the book you want.
Step 2	The computer will probably list several titles. Select the one you want.
Step 3	Read the record to find out if this is the book you want and if the book is available to be checked out.
Step 4	Copy or print out the complete call number for nonfiction books or the author's name and title for fiction books.

Activity C   Use the information in the sample computer record on page 146 to answer these questions. Write your answers on your paper.

1) What is the complete title of the book?
2) Who is the author of the book?
3) Is this book fiction or nonfiction?
4) What is the complete call number of this book?
5) Is a copy of this book available to check out of the library?

The Reference Section

To find specific information, use the reference section of the library. Encyclopedias, atlases, and art books are types of reference books you will often find in the reference section.

Circulate

Can be taken out of the library.

The books in the reference section usually do not **circulate.** This means they cannot be checked out. As a result, these books are always available to the people who need to use them.

Sample Record for a Reference Book

```
R
709
Ja      Art of the western world (ed)
Franco Jackson, Chicago, ArtWorld,
Inc.,
1983
359 p illus


1. Art I.        title          noncirc.
```

Activity D   Use the entry to answer these questions. Write your answers on your paper.

1) What does the *R* on the entry tell you?
2) What was Franco Jackson's job on this book?
3) What is the complete call number for this book?
4) Can you check this book out of the library?

Finding Magazines in the Library

You can find all of the periodicals, or magazines, that your library has in the magazine catalog. A periodical, such as a magazine, is published every week, every month, or at some other regular interval. Each magazine is called an "issue." All of the issues in one year make one "volume."

The **current issue** of a magazine is the most recent issue. It is displayed on a library shelf. A **back issue** is a past issue of a magazine. Some back issues may be kept on the shelves. Usually, issues more than six or twelve months old are kept somewhere else in the library. To look at a back issue, you sometimes must put in a written request. Request forms usually ask for the name of the magazine, the publication date, the volume number, and the issue number.

September 1999 — Month and year of publication

Volume XX — Volume number

Number 9 — Issue number

AUTO NEWS

Driving the new XL301!

Plus

The best buys for 1999 | New auto accessories | AUTO NEWS test drives the new *EuroCar*

Activity E Use the magazine pictured above to answer these questions. Write your answers on your paper.

1) What is the volume number of this magazine?

2) What is the issue number?

3) What is the name of the magazine?

4) When was it published?

The Readers' Guide to Periodical Literature

When you wish to find magazine articles on a specific subject, you can use *The Readers' Guide to Periodical Literature. The Readers' Guide* lists articles and stories from major general interest magazines. Articles are listed by subject and author. Stories are listed by author and title. *The Readers' Guide* is published every month and bound into a volume each year. Some libraries have a guide to magazine articles on computer.

Here are some sample entries in *The Readers' Guide:*

READER'S GUIDE TO PERIODICAL LITERATURE 1999

TRAVEL
    Air travel with 50-foot TV screens.
        B. Howard. il Video Today 13:6-7 Mr. '99
    Moon trips without cheese.
        J. Lee. Short Story Monthly 45:45-67. Ap. '99
TRAVERS, Janice S.
    The Mad Venusian. Tomorrow's Woman. 123:30-46. Ap. '99
    Tunes from another world. Purplebook. 12:24-25. Mr. '99
VIDEO
    What's new in video? News Mag 24:36 il Ap. 11, '99

Activity F   Use the facts in the sample entries above to answer these questions. Write your answers on your paper.

1) What is the title of the article by B. Howard?

2) Which magazine is published weekly?

    a) *Purplebook*

    b) *News Magazine*

    c) *Video Today*

3) How many pages are in the story by J. Lee?

4) What is the volume number of *Tomorrow's Woman* in which Janice Travers's story appears?

5) Does the article "What's New in Video?" have pictures?

Video Catalogs

You can learn about many topics by watching a film, a videocassette, or a videodisc. Not many people have 16mm film projectors at home, but many have videocassette recorders (VCRs). Some have videodisc players. Many libraries have videocassette and videodisc collections. You may be able to check these materials out just like a book.

A video catalog is usually in book form or on a computer system. The materials are grouped by subject. Titles are listed alphabetically. The catalog entries provide facts you might wish to know before you check out or view the work.

READER'S GUIDE TO PERIODICAL LITERATURE 1999

PHYSICAL FITNESS
    Better health through exercise, 1997, 60 min Color VHS.
        (Overnight only.)
    The importance of exercise, 1999. 20 min B&W 16 mm film.
    Suzy Smith's exercise program. 30 min Color VHS.
    You and your health, 1995. 15 min Audiocassette.
        (Lesson guide available)
    Your health today, 60 min 1998, Color videodisc (CED).
        (Library only)

Activity G   Use the information on the video catalog page above to answer these questions. Write your answers on your paper.

1) How many programs are available on videocassette?

2) Which program is available on 16mm film? Write the title.

3) What equipment will you need to watch "Your Health Today"?

4) What equipment will you need to use "You and Your Health"?

5) Which program would have to be returned the day after it is checked out?

6) Which program cannot be checked out of the library?

Activity H   Write the answers to the following questions.

1) What is the title of the film in the film catalog entry below?

> Sports
> > Rules for playing soccer, 1989,
> > b&w, 20 min.

2) How long is this film?

3) In what year was the film produced?

Vertical File

Vertical file
A file that contains pamphlets and other materials too small to put on a shelf.

A **vertical file** is a valuable source of information in the library. It has pamphlets and other material too small or too large to put on a shelf. The vertical file sometimes contains the most current material on a subject. These materials come from a variety of sources, including:

- Government agencies
- Embassies
- Colleges
- Businesses
- Museums
- Organizations

Materials in the vertical file are arranged in alphabetical order according to subject.

USING WHAT YOU HAVE LEARNED

When you go to the library, look up a subject in the vertical file. Use the vertical file the next time you do a report.

Activity I   Which of these materials might be found in the vertical file? Write your answers on your paper.

1) A world almanac

2) A pamphlet on Indiana parks

3) "Growing Vegetables" by the U.S. Department of Agriculture

4) A biography of Malcolm X

5) A road map of your state

6) "A Balanced Diet," 20 pages, published by the Dairy Association

7) A copy of a speech by the town mayor

Part A Use the facts on the cards to answer the questions that follow. Write your answers on your paper.

```
F       SPORTS
Yo      Yount, Nora
           The Wildcats' revenge (by)
        Nora Yount and Frank Sayers,
        Boston. S & T Press. 1980
           132 p illus

        1. Sports.    2. Baseball  I. title
```

```
796.357   SPORTS
Yo        Yount, Nora
             Better baseball (ed) Nora
          Yount, Boston. S & T Press.
          1979
             142 p illus

          1. Sports.    2. Sports history
          3. Baseball      I. title
```

1) What kind of cards are shown—subject, title, or author?

2) What is the title of the book that Nora Yount wrote?

3) What is the title of the book that she edited?

4) What is the call number of the fiction book?

5) In which part of the nonfiction section would you find *Better Baseball*? How do you know?

    a) History   **b)** Arts and Recreation   **c)** Biography

Part B Write your answers to the following questions on your paper.

1) What are the three kinds of records in a library catalog?

2) Which issues of magazines might you have to ask to see?

3) Which of these call numbers are nonfiction?

    Fr   346.03   92   003.1

    F   Ho   Ru   To

4) How are entries in a video catalog usually arranged?

5) Which of these books would be in the reference section?

    a) a literature book **b)** an almanac **c)** a mystery novel

6) Where would you look to find a pamphlet about France?

Part A   Write the answer to these questions on your paper.

1) What is the name of our national library?

2) In what city would you find that library?

3) List two kinds of print materials other than books; two kinds of video equipment; and two other kinds of equipment you might find in the library.

4) In what order would these fiction books be arranged on a library shelf? Write them in order.

   a) *Robinson Crusoe* by Daniel Defoe

   b) *The Outsiders* by S. E. Hinton

   c) *Watership Down* by Richard Adams

5) Which of these types of books are fiction? Which are nonfiction? Make two lists on your paper.

   a) Biography   **e)** History

   b) Autobiography   **f)** Historical novel

   c) Biographical novel   **g)** Short story

   d) Novel   **h)** Article

Part B   Which of the subjects in each group is a main category in the Dewey Decimal system? Write your answers on your paper.

Example   poetry   humor   literature   plays
            Answer: **Literature**

1) travel   climate   biography   history

2) government education   social sciences economics

3) sports   hobbies   recreation   games

4) math   zoology   chemistry   science

5) dictionary grammar   French   language

Part C Write the answer to these questions on your paper.

1) In which section of the library would you look to find the novel *Emma* by Jane Austen?

2) Where would you look to find the most recent issue of *Reader's Digest*?
   a) the vertical file   b) the nonfiction shelf in 300–399
   c) on the magazine display rack

3) Where would you look for a pamphlet about the Falkland Islands?
   a) the reference shelf   b) the vertical file
   c) the nonfiction shelf in 900–999

4) Which of these usually do not circulate in most libraries?
   a) short story collections
   b) books from the reference section

5) What are three kinds of records in the library catalog?

6) According to the call numbers given, is this book fiction or nonfiction?   453.01
                                                        Ty

7) Which of these might be the call number of a biography of Thomas Jefferson by R. Hernandez?
   a) 921   b) 921
      Je   He

8) In what reference book would you look to find a list of magazine articles on a specific subject?

9) Which of these books would probably be in the reference section?
   a) an encyclopedia   b) a historical novel
   c) a literature book

10) Besides title, author, and subject, what are two other pieces of information you might find in a library record?

Test Taking Tip When studying for a test, write your own test questions. Then find a partner and complete each other's tests. Double-check your answers.

Finding Expert Help

What is an expert? An expert is a person who has training and knowledge about a certain subject. An expert may be able to perform a special service for you. For example, an electrician is an expert on electrical wiring. An electrician can install or repair an electrical system.

An expert can also give you advice. For example, an attorney is an expert on matters related to the law. An attorney can give you legal advice or speak for you in a court of law.

In Chapter 6, you will learn how to find expert help. Each lesson will help you know where to go and whom to ask for expert help.

Goals for Learning

▶ To learn how to find expert help when you need it

▶ To learn about nonprofessional experts and how they can help you

▶ To identify organizations that can help you find skilled workers

You can find expert help when you need it. An **expert** is a person who has training and knowledge about a certain subject. An expert has a profession. A profession is a job that requires special information and often long training. Examples of professionals are architects, engineers, physicians, attorneys, and pharmacists.

A person who is considered to be an expert has certain professional **credentials**. Credentials are proof that a person is an expert in a certain **occupation**. An occupation is the regular work or business of an individual.

A person's credentials may include these things:

- A college degree in a certain field

- A degree from a professional school

- A license or certificate

- Experience or references

Understanding College Degrees

Colleges and universities offer different degrees which acknowledge that a person has studied in a particular subject area, such as math or science. Various degrees require different numbers of years of study.

> **Associate's Degree:** A degree from a two-year college or a community college. For example:
>
> A.A.—Associate in Arts
>
> **Bachelor's Degree:** A degree from a four-year college or university. Many professional occupations require this degree. The most common of these degrees are
>
> B.A.—Bachelor of Arts
>
> B.S.—Bachelor of Science

Master's Degree: A degree from a graduate school or a university. This degree means that the person has had advanced training after a bachelor's degree. Some examples are

    M.Ed.—Master of Education

    M.B.A.—Master of Business Administration

    M.S.—Master of Science

Doctoral Degree: The highest degree that a university or professional school may award. Many medical professionals must have this degree. Many professors in colleges and universities have this degree. Some examples are

    M.D.—Doctor of Medicine

    Ph.D.—Doctor of Philosophy

    D.V.M.—Doctor of Veterinary Medicine

Activity A   Match the degree with the best definition. Write each number and matching letter on your paper.

1) Associate degree   **a)** Awarded by four-year colleges or universities

2) Bachelor's degree   **b)** The highest degree a person can receive in a field

3) Master's degree   **c)** Awarded by community colleges

4) Doctoral degree   **d)** Awarded by graduate schools

Activity B   Here are some abbreviations of credentials. Use a dictionary to find out what each abbreviation means. Write their meanings on your paper.

1) M.A.   **6)** B.F.A.

2) J.D.   **7)** LL.B.

3) R.N.   **8)** L.P.N.

4) C.P.A.   **9)** Ed.D.

5) D.D.S.   **10)** D.V.M.

Professional Schools

Professional schools provide training for certain occupations. For example, a lawyer must graduate from a law school, and a doctor must graduate from a medical school. Often these schools are part of a large university. Most students receive a bachelor's degree before they attend professional schools.

Becoming a Professional

Professionals usually graduate from a college or a professional school and sometimes from both. Then they must get experience. Finally, they must take an examination. State governments give these exams. They are called State Board Examinations. A person who passes the examination receives a license to practice the profession.

On the wall in your physician's office you may see several degrees to show his or her credentials. They probably include:

- An undergraduate degree from a college or university.

- A degree from a medical school.

- A license to practice medicine in the state where the physician practices.

Activity C   A person must do the following things to become a professional. Arrange the steps in the order they are usually done. Write them in order on your paper.

1) Get experience under the supervision of another expert.

2) Pass a state board examination.

3) Graduate from a professional school.

4) Graduate from high school.

5) Attend a four-year college or university.

Business and Financial Experts

There are many experts you may go to for advice and service in business and financial matters. Here are some examples:

Bankers loan people money for automobiles, houses, and other purchases. Many bankers have college degrees and years of experience working at various jobs in banking.

Real estate agents and brokers help people buy, sell, and rent property. Agents and brokers must have a license. A broker has more training and experience than an agent. Agents and brokers must pass state examinations.

Accountants prepare financial reports for businesses. They help people with their taxes. They check financial reports to be sure they are correct. Most accountants have college degrees. Some accountants become certified public accountants or C.P.A.s. An accountant must have experience and pass a state examination to become a C.P.A.

Attorneys, or lawyers, graduate from law school. Then they must take a state examination called a bar exam. After they pass this exam, attorneys may practice law in a court and represent other people in court. They can draw up legal papers such as wills and contracts and give advice to people about the law.

Architects graduate from college. Then they must get experience. Finally, they can take a state examination to become certified. Architects design homes and other buildings.

Architects must study math, design, and engineering to do their jobs well.

Activity D   Use the information on page 161 to answer these questions. Write your answers on your paper.

1) What does C.P.A. stand for?
2) What is the name of the examination attorneys must pass?
3) Which person has more training and experience—a real estate agent or a real estate broker?
4) What kind of professional helps you borrow money for a car or house?
5) Does an architect need a license or certificate to practice his or her profession?

As Mrs. Sabatino's business grows, she consults different professionals to help her with banking, taxes, and buying a second restaurant.

Activity E   Mrs. Rose Sabatino owns a pizza restaurant. On your paper, write the kind of professional who can help Mrs. Sabatino with each of the problems described below.

1) Mrs. Sabatino has been selling a lot of pizzas. She needs a bigger kitchen. She would like to borrow some money.
2) Mrs. Sabatino thinks she is paying too much in taxes every year.
3) Mrs. Sabatino has been thinking about opening another restaurant. She has found a location but would like to know more about the area.
4) Mrs. Sabatino's son suggested that she have a second restaurant built. She would like to see some designs before making a decision.
5) Mrs. Sabatino would like to know about the legal aspects of becoming a corporation.

Physicians and Surgeons

There are many kinds of physicians, or medical doctors. Some of these physicians are general practitioners, or family doctors. Other physicians are specialists in certain areas.

EXAMPLES	Name of Specialist	Area of Special Training
	Allergist	Allergies
	Cardiologist	Heart
	Dermatologist	Skin disorders
	Internist	Diseases that do not require surgery
	Obstetrician	Pregnancy and childbirth
	Oncologist	Cancer
	Ophthalmologist	Eyes
	Orthopedist	Bones, joints, and muscles
	Otolaryngologist	Ear, nose, and throat
	Pediatrician	Infants and children
	Psychiatrist	Nervous or mental disorders
	Radiologist	High-energy radiation (X-rays)
	Surgeon	Surgery (operations)

Activity F Which kind of specialist could help with each of these problems? Write your answers on your paper.

1) Mr. Lopez hurt his eye.

2) Jim has a skin rash.

3) Marta has an earache.

4) Mrs. Rosen starts sneezing every time she is near a cat.

5) Mrs. Tsao is pregnant.

6) Leon sprained his ankle playing basketball.

7) Mr. Franklin is depressed and cannot sleep.

8) Ted has to have his appendix removed.

9) Mr. and Mrs. Ashike's baby has a fever.

10) Liz needs a complete physical examination for college.

Other Medical Professionals

Many medical professionals have degrees from a professional school. However, they are not medical doctors. Each of these professionals must pass a state examination to receive a license to practice.

Podiatrists are doctors of podiatric medicine. They specialize in problems related to feet.

Pharmacists fill prescriptions that medical doctors write. They work in drug stores and pharmacies. A doctoral degree is not required for this job.

Dentists are doctors of dental surgery. They treat teeth and gums. They may write prescriptions.

Chiropractors treat people by manipulating the spinal column. They prescribe diet, exercise, and rest. They do not write prescriptions or perform surgery.

Optometrists examine eyes and write prescriptions for glasses. They do not treat injuries or perform surgery.

Veterinarians treat animals and perform surgery if needed. They also can prescribe medicines for animals.

Activity G Which kind of medical professional could help with each of these problems? Write your answers on your paper.

1) Della's gums are sore.

2) Carolyn's cat won't eat.

3) Aunt Julia needs a prescription filled.

4) Joey is having trouble seeing the blackboard from his seat in the back of the classroom.

5) Mr. Williams's back is aching.

6) Steve has an ingrown toenail.

Part A   Write the answers to these questions on your paper.

1) Which of these degrees does a community college give?

   a) bachelor's   **b)** associate's   **c)** master's

2) What is the highest degree a college or university can give?

   a) bachelor's   **b)** master's   **c)** doctoral

3) What type of professional worker can receive a C.P.A.?

   a) banker   **b)** accountant   **c)** attorney

4) Which of these health professionals is a medical doctor?

   a) chiropractor   **b)** podiatrist   **c)** allergist

5) What kind of examination does a lawyer take?

   a) C.P.A. exam   **b)** bar exam   **c)** medical exam

Part B   Which professional does the person in each situation need? Write the letter of the correct answer on your paper.

1) Mr. and Mrs. Weber want to draw up a will.

   a) attorney   **b)** accountant   **c)** podiatrist

2) Aunt Lynn needs to have a filling replaced.

   a) allergist   **b)** chiropractor   **c)** dentist

3) Alan Fowler's hamster is sick.

   a) pediatrician   **b)** veterinarian   **c)** pharmacist

4) Paul Carter wants to start a business. He needs a loan.

   a) banker   **b)** accountant   **c)** real estate agent

5) Anna Walters needs help with her taxes.

   a) attorney   **b)** accountant   **c)** real estate broker

6) Aunt Harriet broke her arm.

   a) orthopedist   **b)** podiatrist   **c)** dermatologist

7) Susanna Choy needs a chest x-ray.

   a) radiologist   **b)** cardiologist   **c)** surgeon

Experts learn their skills in many different ways. They may attend technical or vocational schools, or they may go to business schools. They may participate in apprenticeship programs or get on-the-job training.

Becoming an Expert

Skilled workers develop skills through a combination of training and experience.

1. They go to school to learn facts about the work.
2. They get experience on the job where they are carefully supervised by an experienced person. This applies to both professionals and nonprofessionals.

> **EXAMPLES**   An intern is a recent medical school graduate who practices medicine under the supervision of an experienced doctor.
>
> An apprentice is someone who is learning a trade, such as plumbing, under the supervision of a licensed plumber.

3. After the training period, workers usually take an examination. The exam may be written, oral, or practical.
4. Workers are then allowed to do their jobs on their own. They still have a boss, but they are not closely supervised.

Activity A   Write a definition for each of the following on your paper.

1) apprentice

2) intern

3) professional

4) nonprofessional

5) expert

Apprentice
A worker being trained by an experienced and skilled person.

Contractor
A person who agrees to perform work or to provide supplies for a job.

Foreman
A supervisor or boss.

Independent contractors
People in business for themselves.

Journeyman
A worker who has completed an apprenticeship and passed a test.

Master's level
A worker who has more experience than a journeyman and has passed another test. This worker has earned a master's license.

Trade
An occupation that requires manual or mechanical skill.

Choosing an Expert

There is more than one way to get a job done. You can do it yourself. You can find a friend to help you. You can hire an expert. People often hire other experts to do work for them, such as cutting hair or fixing a television set. When you hire an expert to do a job, you have the right to expect expert work. To ensure that you receive expert work, be sure to check the person's credentials. Remember that credentials are proof that the person has been trained to do the job.

Credentials can include these things:

- A license issued by your state government
- A certificate or degree from a school
- Recommendations from other people
- A written guarantee from the worker

Experts in the Trades

A **trade** is an occupation that requires manual or mechanical skill. Examples are plumber, electrician, carpenter, auto mechanic, and printer.

An **apprentice** is a worker who is learning from an experienced and skilled person.

A **journeyman** has completed an apprenticeship and passed a test.

A **master's level** worker has more experience than a journeyman and has passed another test. This worker has a master's license.

A **foreman** is a supervisor or boss.

A **contractor** agrees to perform work or to provide supplies. Contractors may not be skilled workers themselves, but they hire other people with skills.

Independent contractors are people in business for themselves. They do not work for just one company or corporation.

Think about the skilled people who have helped you. List the names of their occupations and what they did. Share your list with your classmates. Do not list professional workers such as doctors.

Example

Tailor: Altered my new suit.

Activity B Write on your paper the missing words to complete these sentences. Refer to page 167.

1) A plumber, a printer, and a carpenter each have a _____ .

2) An _____ is a worker who is learning a skill from someone with more experience or credentials.

3) Contractors agree to perform _____ .

4) A foreman is a _____ or _____ .

5) A worker who has completed an apprenticeship is a _____ .

6) A journeyman must take another test to receive a _____ license.

Activity C Read about these workers. Then write on your paper the answers to the questions on page 169.

a) Mr. Johnson repairs appliances such as washing machines and stoves. He goes to people's houses to do his work. He has an apprentice who helps him.

b) The Franklin Appliance Company sells appliances. You can also hire the company to fix appliances. Skilled workers and apprentices work there.

c) Ralph Attaway is a piano tuner. He was an apprentice at the Fine Music Store for four years. Now he is in business for himself. He will come to your house to tune or repair your piano.

d) Carlotta Rios is an emergency medical technician. She works for the fire department. You can get her help by calling for the Rescue Squad. Her training included special medical emergency courses and many hours of experience.

e) Fred Collins works for Mac's Service Station. He is an auto mechanic. He was an apprentice to an auto dealer for four years. Now he is a head mechanic. There are two part-time workers who help him.

f) Andrea Brown is an air conditioning specialist. She works for Young's Heating and Air Conditioning, Inc. Her company sent her to evening classes for several years. Now she trains new workers.

1) Which worker does not charge a fee for services?

2) Which workers are independent contractors?

3) If you hire Fred Collins to repair your car, who is actually responsible for his work—Fred or Mac's Service Station?

4) Where did Ralph Attaway work as an apprentice?

5) Andrea Brown trains new workers. What is the name for these workers?

Activity D   Choose an expert from the list to help with each problem described below. Write your answers on your paper.

auto mechanic	barber	auto body mechanic
beautician	baker	ironworker
roofer	jeweler	tilesetter
travel agent	surveyor	watchmaker
locksmith	musician	firefighter

1) Sandy wants an expert to cut and color her hair.

2) Harold Williams had an accident with his car. His fender is dented. He needs someone who is skilled in this kind of repair work.

3) Lyn wants to fly to Chicago. She could call an airline herself, or she could call someone to make reservations for her.

4) Jane Anderson wants to order a wedding cake.

5) Mrs. West bought a ring that is too small. She needs to have it made larger.

6) Mr. Cosby locked his keys inside his car and cannot get them out.

7) Kim Williams admired her sister's tile floor. Now Kim wants new flooring in her bathroom.

8) The Andersons' roof is leaking.

9) The Rosen family found a lot of land they really like. Before they buy it, they must find a worker who can measure the land and mark the boundaries.

10) The Garcias want to hire a good dance band for their daughter's wedding.

Part A Choose the best answer for each item. Write the letter of your answer on your paper.

1) A plumber who is learning the trade is

   a) a journeyman.   b) an apprentice.   c) an intern.

2) The most skilled craftsperson is a

   a) journeyman.   b) master craftsworker.   c) contractor.

3) Which of the following can be considered credentials?

   a) a license   c) a written guarantee

   b) a recommendation   d) all of the above

4) Which worker can help you plan a trip?

   a) a jeweler   b) a travel agent   c) a locksmith

5) Which worker must go to college to learn the job?

   a) an insurance agent   c) a jeweler

   b) a travel agent   d) none of the above

6) What is true about independent contractors?

   a) They work for more than one company.

   b) They have more experience than other contractors.

   c) They do not need a special license.

Part B Write your responses to each item.

1) Name at least two ways that you can identify an expert.

2) Here is a list of the steps needed to become an expert in a trade. Write these steps in order on your paper.

   • Become a journeyman.

   • Get a master's license.

   • Become an apprentice.

You already have learned one important skill to help you find expert help. You can use the Yellow Pages of your telephone directory. You have also learned ways to check for the credentials experts should have.

Organization

A group of people united for a common cause.

There is another way to check the credentials of people you wish to hire. You can get help from **organizations** or **bureaus**. An organization is a group of people united for a common cause. A bureau is a specialized group or department that focuses on one main topic.

Look at the following list of organizations and bureaus. You or a member of your family may have received help from one or more of them sometime in the past.

Bureau

A specialized group or department that focuses on one area or one main topic.

> The Medical Bureau
> The Better Business Bureau
> Welcome Wagon
> The Chamber of Commerce
> Travelers Aid Society
> The Legal Aid Society
> The Consumers Union

Organizations and How They Can Help

1. **The Medical Bureau or the Medical Society**

   If you need a doctor, this group can help. Representatives can give names of doctors near your home who are taking new patients.

2. **The Better Business Bureau**

People at the Better Business Bureau can help by giving you information about the services and service record of a certain company. You can use your own judgment about whether to use the company or not. You can find the telephone number of the Better Business Bureau in the telephone directory.

BETTER BUSINESS BUREAU OF YOUR CITY
General Information 1223 Main St ·································· **454-9000**
Complaint Service 1223 Main St ·································· **454-9020**

3. **Welcome Wagon or Welcome, Neighbor**

Your neighbors can also help you settle into a new home.

If you are new in town, you can call a group that welcomes people to the community. Local businesses support these groups. Groups like the Welcome Wagon give facts about shopping, schools, hospitals, and doctors in your town.

4. The Chamber of Commerce

Business people from the community belong to this organization. You can write to the Chamber of Commerce of any city or town in the United States to request information about places to visit, hotels, restaurants, and other businesses in the city or town.

5. Travelers Aid or Travelers Assistance

If you are visiting a new place and need help with a problem, you can call this group. For example, if you lose your wallet or need to find a doctor, this kind of group may be able to help. However, a group such as Travelers Aid is not a travel agent. Look for this organization in the telephone book or call the operator for help.

6. The Legal Aid Society

Attorneys at the Legal Aid Society will answer your questions on the telephone. They will agree to see you in person for a fee. They may also recommend another attorney who can help you with your problem.

7. The Consumers Union

Consumer

Someone who buys and uses goods and services.

A **consumer** is a person who buys and uses goods and services. The **Consumers Union** is an organization that tests products and investigates businesses. It publishes the results in a magazine called *Consumer Reports*. You can find this magazine in most libraries.

Consumers Union

A group that tests products and investigates businesses. The Consumers Union publishes the results of its tests in a magazine called Consumer Reports.

Your town or city may also have a consumers' group. This group would report about businesses in your area. You may find the name and telephone number in your directory. Your librarian should know about consumer groups.

Find the telephone number for one of the groups listed on pages 171–173. Call the group and ask for information. Ask the person who answers to send you whatever printed information is available. Prepare a report about the group for your class.

Activity A Use the information on pages 171–173 to answer these questions. Write your answers on your paper.

1) Which group would you call for the name of a pediatrician in your town?

2) Which group would you call to ask if there have been any complaints about Mac's Service Station?

3) What organization could help if you were traveling in a new city and had a problem?

4) What organization would you call for legal advice?

5) What is a group that gives information to people who are new in town?

6) What organization helps businesses in the community?

Lesson Review Number your paper 1 to 10. Read about each person's problem and write the name of the group or organization that might help solve that problem. There may be more than one right answer for each question.

1) Justin wants a new car. He would like to know the price of compact cars. He also wants to know some facts about each one.

2) Mrs. Okada needs an attorney to help her with business.

3) Nick's doctor retired. Nick would like to find a new doctor. Nick wants the office to be near his house.

4) The Sanapaws are new in town. They would like information about the community.

5) Jack Bevan is planning a trip to Los Angeles, California. He would like to know about interesting places to visit while he is there.

6) Trisha Earle wants to have her washing machine repaired. John's Small Appliance Store is listed in the Yellow Pages. Trisha wants to find out if that business is reliable.

7) Uncle Jonathan needs new glasses. He wants the name of an optometrist.

8) Sam Young went to Wilkinsburg on business. He lost his wallet.

9) Mary Franklin is buying a vacuum cleaner. She wants to know which is the most reliable model.

10) The Home Improvement Company has called Mrs. Condelli. The company wants to sell her new storm doors and windows. She wants to check on their reputation.

Part A   Choose the letter of the correct answer. Write it on your paper.

1) Which of these professionals is a medical doctor?

    a) optometrist   **b)** pharmacist   **c)** pediatrician

2) Which expert will help you find information on any subject?

    a) lawyer   **b)** librarian   **c)** accountant

3) Which degree is the highest that a university can award?

    a) A.A.   **b)** Ph.D.   **c)** C.P.A.

4) Which professional must pass a state board examination?

    a) accountant   **b)** librarian   **c)** attorney

5) Which professional can help you buy, sell, or rent a house?

    a) plumber   **b)** real estate broker   **c)** lawyer

6) Which credential should a nonprofessional worker have?

    a) a college degree   **b)** proof of skills or training

7) What is the name of a worker who is learning a trade?

    a) apprentice   **b)** journeyman   **c)** foreman

8) Which worker will help you plan a trip?

    a) pharmacist   **b)** travel agent   **c)** intern

9) Which of these is a credential?

    a) a big ad   **b)** recommendation   **c)** a bright sign

10) Which worker may not have special skills for a job but hires other workers who do have the skills?

    a) contractor   **b)** apprentice   **c)** journeyman

Part B   When you have a problem, you need to know the kind of expert that can help. Number your paper 1 to 5. Write the kind of expert that can help with each problem. Use the *Experts* list below.

Problems

1) Sal's car is making a funny noise.

2) Donna's cat, Larson, needs his annual shots.

3) Robert wonders if there is a book about repairing air conditioners.

4) Floyd has a stain on his new suit.

5) Kenesha needs some medicine for poison ivy.

Experts

librarian

pharmacist

mechanic

dry cleaner

veterinarian

Part C   Write on your paper your answers to these questions.

1) Which organization can give you legal advice?

2) Which organization helps people who are new to a city?

3) Which organization publishes a magazine that reports on products and services?

4) Which organization can tell you if a company has been reliable in the past?

5) If you needed a doctor, which group could you call?

Test Taking Tip

If you know you will have to define certain terms on a test, write the term on one side of a card. Write its definition on the other side. Use the cards to test yourself, or work with a partner.

Chapter 7

Information From the Media

W hen someone has a message for one or two people, a letter or a telephone call is the best means of communication. When someone has a message for the general public, the best means of communication is mass media. Mass media, which includes television, radio, newspapers, and magazines, reaches the most people at one time.

In Chapter 7, you will learn about three types of media: newspapers, television, and radio. Each lesson focuses on the characteristics of the different types of media and how you can use them to find information.

Goals for Learning

▶ To learn about information from three types of media: newspapers, television, and radio

▶ To learn about the parts of a newspaper

▶ To learn about reading a newspaper for information

▶ To learn how to use the classified advertising section

▶ To learn how to use the help wanted section of the classified ads

▶ To learn how to use television and radio for information

Current
Up to the present.

Daily
Every day.

Local
Having to do with one certain place.

Mass media
A way to communicate with the most people at one time; for example, television, radio, newspapers, and magazines.

National
Having to do with a whole country, or nation.

Newspapers are part of the **mass media**. Everyone who reads a newspaper receives the same information. There are two main kinds of newspapers: **daily** and weekly. Daily newspapers are published and distributed every day. They have the most **current**, or up-to-the-present, news. They usually have more **national** and world news than weekly papers. National news has to do with what's happening in a nation. Generally, daily newspapers have more regular readers than weekly papers. Weekly newspapers often are published in small towns. They usually focus on **local** news. Local news has to do with one certain place.

Parts of a Newspaper and Kinds of News

Newspapers are divided into parts, or sections. Each part has a different kind of news: national and world news, local news, sports news, business news, regular features, and classified advertisements, or ads. Although all newspapers are organized in slightly different ways, many follow a similar plan.

- Articles about national and world news appear in the front section of most large city newspapers. They usually continue to another page or section of the newspaper. Local newspapers that serve suburbs of large cities may not carry national and world news.

- Local news is information about local events of interest. Local news is often placed in a special section of the newspaper. Sometimes it follows the national and world news section. Local news may also be called regional news.

- Sports news is information about sports. Most newspapers have a special sports section. These pages have results from recent sporting events, articles about sports personalities, and general sports news.

- Business news is information about the stock market and events affecting businesses large and small. Many newspapers have a separate section for business news.

- Regular features are **columns** and articles with information of interest to the public, such as gardening, health, advice, or celebrities. Comics, television and movie schedules, and announcements about weddings and engagements are included in the regular features of the newspaper.

- **Classified advertisements**, or ads, are short public notices that offer items for sale. This section of the paper includes houses for sale, apartments for rent, and the help wanted ads that announce available jobs. People pay money to place an ad in the classified section of the newspaper. Classified ads are a source of income for the newspaper publishers. Additional money to run the paper comes from newspaper sales and subscriptions and from the sales of advertisements.

Activity A   Use the information that begins on page 180 to answer these questions. Write your answers on your paper.

1) Which type of news would you expect to find on the front pages of a big city newspaper?

    a) world news   **c)** sports news

    b) local news   **d)** business news

2) Which section of the paper would you check to find the score of last night's basketball game?

    a) classified advertisements   **c)** front page

    b) business news   **d)** sports section

3) Which section of the paper would you check for information about used computers for sale?

    a) business section   **c)** classified advertisements

    b) sports section   **d)** feature section

4) Which section of the newspaper would you check for information about a company that was sold?

    a) business section   **c)** national news

    b) sports section   **d)** regular features

Editorial Pages

The **editorial** section of the paper often appears on the last two pages of the front section of the newspaper. Editorials express opinions about events in the news. The people who write them work for the newspaper. The editorial pages also usually have letters to the editor, political cartoons, and opinion columns.

Letters to the editor are written by people who read the newspaper. Anyone may write a letter to the editor of any newspaper. The letters are often opinions of the readers in response to editorials, feature articles, columns, and even photographs printed in the newspaper.

Political cartoons show an artist's opinion about current events.

A column is a regular newspaper feature. Columns tell about recent events, current political and social issues, and other topics of interest to readers. Columns are written by professional writers called **columnists**. Columnists explain events and issues in the news from their points of view. They often give their opinions about how problems can be solved.

Activity B   Use the information given above to answer these questions. Write your answers on your paper.

1) Where will you usually find the editorial pages in a newspaper?

2) What kinds of information will you find in the editorial section of the newspaper?

3) What is the purpose of an editorial?

4) Who writes the letters to the editor and why?

5) What do columnists write about?

Other Parts of a Newspaper

Newspapers contain many other kinds of information. For example, the television programming directory is a feature that lists the names, times, and channels of programs scheduled for viewing that day. The movie section of the newspaper lists all of the movie theaters in the area with the names of current movies

Cartoon
Usually a single drawing that the artist uses to tell a joke or express an idea.

Comic strip
A series of cartoon frames that tell a story.

Death notice
Information about a person's death and details about the funeral arrangements.

Obituary
A short article about someone who has recently died.

and show times. Information about television programs, movies, and other arts and entertainment events is often placed in a separate section of the paper. This section may be titled *Living, Arts & Entertainment,* or simply *Entertainment.*

Obituaries and **death notices** are included in another section. This section may be called *Obituaries* or *Deaths.* An obituary is a brief article about someone who has recently died. A death notice gives information about a person's death and funeral arrangements.

Columns related to fashion, sports, television, new movies, bridge, chess, gardening, or health can be found in different sections of the newspaper. Some columnists give advice to readers about how to improve some aspect of their lives.

Comic strips and **cartoons** can be found in a special section of the newspaper called the comics. A comic strip is a series of cartoons that tell a story. A cartoon is usually a single drawing that the artist uses to tell a joke or express an idea.

Activity C   Use the information on page 182 and above to answer these questions. Write your answer on your paper.

1) José wants to see a movie at a local theater. Which part of the newspaper will tell him what time the movie begins?

2) Marie enjoys the reruns of the old television program *M*A*S*H.* What newspaper feature would tell her when it is on?

3) Which part of the paper lists the names of people who have recently died?

4) Eddie enjoys the cartoon characters in "Peanuts." In which section of the paper should he look to read about their latest adventures?

Lesson 1 Review

Part A Use any newspaper for this activity. Find each of the following parts of the newspaper.

1) National and world news
2) Local news
3) Columns
4) Sports news
5) Television and movies

6) Classified ads
7) Comics
8) Editorial page
9) Obituaries
10) Business news

Part B Copy the following list of terms on your paper. Beside each term, write the letter of its meaning.

Terms

1) Editorial
2) Daily
3) Regular feature
4) Mass media
5) Classified ad
6) National news
7) Current event
8) Obituary
9) Local news
10) Columnist

Meanings

a) A way to get information to many people at one time

b) A very recent happening

c) Happening every day

d) An event of interest to people in a whole country

e) An event of interest to people in a certain area

f) A list of automobiles, houses, and other things for sale or rent

g) An article about someone who has just died

h) A writer who gives personal opinions

i) An item that appears in every issue

j) An opinion about a current event or issue

In Lesson 1, you learned about daily and weekly newspapers. Daily newspapers have the most up-to-date, or current, world, national, and regional news. A weekly paper usually contains more local news that is of interest to a smaller number of people.

Activity A   Number your paper 1 to 5. Decide whether you would be more likely to look in a daily paper or a local weekly paper to find the answer to each of the following questions. Write *Daily* or *Local* beside each number on your paper.

1) What time will the high school production of *West Side Story* begin Friday evening?

2) Did the president meet with other world leaders to discuss ways to preserve our environment?

3) Who won the city championship in baseball last week?

4) What are the win-loss records of teams in the National Football Conference?

5) When is the Calverton City Council's next meeting?

The Newspaper Index

Most newspapers have an index on the front page or the second page. You can use the index to quickly locate the pages on which the different sections of the paper begin.

INDEX			
Business	C-9	Living	D-1
Classified	C-18	Local	B-1
Comics	B-9	Movies	D-4
Deaths	B-6	Sports	C-1
Editorials	A-26	TV/Radio	D-8
Food	E-1	Weather	B-10

Activity B Use the index on page 185 to locate the page on which you would find each of these items. Write your answers on your paper.

1) Comic strips

2) A political cartoon

3) Scores of last night's basketball game

4) The time a funeral will be held for someone who recently died

5) "Dear Abby" or "Ann Landers"

6) The time and channel of a TV program

7) Recipes and food store advertisements

8) News about local events

9) A list of used cars for sale

10) The damage caused by yesterday's storm

11) A letter to the editor

12) The movies that are playing at your local movie theater

13) How the stock market did yesterday

14) Apartments for rent

15) What the weather will be like tomorrow across your state.

Choosing What to Read

Some people read the daily newspaper from cover to cover. Others skim the paper, looking for specific articles and information. For example, some people may wish to know the results of yesterday's state elections. Others may want to find the coupon for free admission to the Science Museum's new exhibit. Some may wish to read a review of the new Mexican restaurant on Main Street. Investors may look in the business or financial section of the paper for information on the stock market. Recent high-school and college graduates might turn to the help wanted ads to find out what jobs are available in the area. Sports fans may look in the sports section to find out when the Harlem Globetrotters will be in town.

News Stories

Reporter

A person who researches facts and writes stories for a newspaper.

Editor

A person who decides which stories will be reported to the public.

Lead

The first paragraph of a news story; summarizes the most important facts in the story and answers the questions Who? What? Where? *and* When?

News stories are the result of the combined efforts of newspaper **reporters** and their **editors**. A reporter finds facts and writes stories, or articles, for a newspaper. An editor decides which stories will be reported to the public. An editor also may rearrange and correct the information in a reporter's story.

Most news stories begin with a strong first paragraph called a **lead**. The lead is a summary of the most important facts in the story. It answers the questions *Who? What? Where?* and *When?* Other paragraphs in the story explain more about the news event and also answer questions: *Why did the event happen? How did the event happen?*

Reporters arrange facts and details in paragraphs in order of importance. They usually put the least important facts in the last paragraph. Editors know how much space is available for each story. When there is not enough room for the entire story, an editor may cut the last paragraphs.

Activity C   Read the news story below. Then write your answers to the questions that follow on your paper.

Sabatino to Open Pizza Parlor

Beginning Wednesday, March 8, you can eat Rosa Sabatino's pizza at a new location. Rosa's Pizza Parlor is opening in the Fairmont Shopping Center. In her announcement, Mrs. Sabatino said that the demand for her pizza had outgrown her original small kitchen and she had to open a larger facility.

1) Who is the story about?

2) What will happen?

3) When will it happen?

4) Why is it happening?

5) Where will the event take place?

Activity D   Read this news story. Then write on your paper your answers to the questions that follow.

"Welcome, Neighbor" Opens Office

As of April 3, Calverton will have its own "Welcome, Neighbor" with offices in the Rolling Hills Mall. Anyone new to town can call Sharon Imai, director, at 455-0980.

Imai stated that there was a need for a Calverton branch of the group because of the new townhouse development in Calverton. More than 200 new families will be moving into the area during the next year.

"Welcome, Neighbor" offers information about schools, churches, businesses, doctors, and hospitals. Local business people and other groups who wish to help should call Imai weekdays, between 9 A.M. and 3 P.M.

1) What facts are presented in the lead paragraph?

2) Who is Sharon Imai?

3) Why was there a need for a "Welcome, Neighbor" in Calverton?

4) How can someone get help from this group?

5) What does "Welcome, Neighbor" do for people new to town?

6) Where will the Calverton branch of "Welcome, Neighbor" be?

7) When will the branch open?

8) List some other facts or details that are in this story.

Getting Information From Advertisements

A newspaper earns money in two ways. First, people buy the newspaper. Second, people pay to have their **advertisements** printed. An advertisement is a public notice, often about something for sale. Newspaper ads also give you information that you might find useful.

Grand Opening!

Rosa's Pizza Parlor

When? Wednesday, March 8

Where? Fairmont Shopping Center

CLIP THIS COUPON

Buy one large Pizza Supreme at regular price and GET ONE Rosa's LARGE CHEESE PIZZA

FREE!

OFFER GOOD UNTIL MARCH 18

Activity E   Write on your paper your answers to these questions about the ad for Rosa's Pizza Parlor.

1) How will the advertisement help Rosa's Pizza Parlor?

2) When will Rosa's Pizza Parlor open for business?

3) Where is the Pizza Parlor located?

4) What do you have to do to get a free pizza?

5) When will the coupon offer end?

6) What information about the pizza supreme is missing?

Advertisements often have **gimmicks** and **slogans** that can mislead consumers. A gimmick is an important feature about something that is kept secret. It is also called a catch.

A slogan is a word or phrase expressing the main idea of a product, business, political group, or other organization. Businesses repeat their slogans over and over again.

EXAMPLE

Dawson's Department Store
"The Store for Men"

Winter Coat Sale!

100s of coats!

All styles and sizes!

$13495 *and up.*

Darby Mall, Main and 5th

Tire Sale!

The **AUTO CENTER**

"The place to go for all your auto needs!"

BEST BUY!
$79 00 *radials*
reduced to **$54**00

1245 W. Tulip Drive

Activity F Study the two ads. Then write on your paper your answers to the following questions.

1) What is the slogan of Dawson's Department Store?

2) List the facts in the Dawson ad.

3) What important piece of information is missing about the price of the coats? Why does this make the ad misleading?

4) What is the slogan of The Auto Center?

5) List the facts in the Auto Center ad.

6) What is a possible gimmick in the Auto Center ad?

Part A Write on your paper your answers to these questions.

1) What six questions do newspaper stories usually answer?

2) Which newspaper worker is responsible for finding the facts and writing the story?

3) Who decides which stories to print?

4) Which paragraph of the news story tells the main facts?

5) What are some reasons why people usually read the newspaper?

6) How often are local newspapers usually published?

7) How often are large city newspapers usually published?

8) Where could you look to find out on which page the sports section of the newspaper begins?

Part B Write on your paper your answers to these questions.

1) Name two ways that newspapers make money.

2) What is an advertisement?

3) What kind of information do ads contain?

4) How can ads mislead people?

5) Give an example of a slogan. It can be an actual slogan or one you make up.

Advertise

To announce something to the public through the media.

Large businesses use newspaper ads, television, radio, and magazines to **advertise** their products and services. To advertise means to announce to the public by printed notice or broadcast.

There may be a time when you want to advertise something. You may have something you want to sell, or you may be running a business and looking for help. You can reach a lot of people at one time if you advertise in the classified ads in daily and weekly newspapers. When things are classified, they are divided into groups. In the classified section of the newspaper, short announcements about job openings or items for sale are arranged, or classified, into sections. Often there will be an index at the beginning of the classified ads that lists each section. Usually there will be guide words or numbers or both at the top of each column to help people find what they are looking for quickly.

CLASSIFIED INDEX

100 – 199	Announcements and Notices
200 – 299	Personal and Business Services
300 – 399	Recreation and Leisure
400 – 499	Gourmet and Hosting
500 – 599	Home Repairs and Services
600 – 699	Pets and Animals
700 – 799	Merchandise
800 – 899	Instruction
900 – 999	Employment
1000 – 1099	Rentals
1100 – 1199	Real Estate
1200 – 1299	Business and Business Real Estate
1300 – 1399	Financial
1400 – 1499	Transportation

To advertise in most papers, you will have to pay a fee. The amount of the fee will depend on the size of your ad. Some papers have special programs that charge a fee only after your ad gets results.

Activity A   Use the Classified Index on page 192 to answer these questions. Write the numbers and the title of each topic on your paper.

1) Under which classification would you find a truck for sale?

2) Under which classification would you expect to find a house for sale?

3) Where would you expect to find job openings?

4) Where would you look if you wanted to get a cat?

5) If you wanted to take a class, what would you look under?

Activity B   Sort the following advertisements into two sections that you might see in the classified ads in the newspaper—*Furniture* and *Business Equipment*. Write *F* on your paper if an item should be listed in the Furniture section or *BE* if the item should be listed in the Business Equipment section.

BEDROOM SET New $1995. Moving; must sacrifice. $650 or best offer. 238-4212.

SOFA Green brushed twill in good condition. $650. Call 345-0984. Ask for Marlene.

CASH REGISTER New in sealed carton, $129. Calvert Cash Register Co. 567-0900.

DESK AND CHAIR Solid wood. Good condition, $450. Call evenings. 399-4039.

COPIERS Reconditioned. All sizes. Like new. Bargain priced $399 and up. Call 320-4835 between 8 and 5.

DINETTE, RECLINER, LAMPS, and more. We're moving south and everything must go. Call 430-9864.

Placing Classified Ads

If you place a classified ad in the paper, you want people to find it. You want people to know what you are selling or advertising. The classified ad operator can help you write the ad and place it in the most appropriate section of the classifieds.

EXAMPLES   Mr. Sanchez wanted to buy a used piano. He looked under Merchandise (things for sale). First, he looked for the word *Piano*. Then he looked for the words *Musical Instruments.* He found a piano for sale.

Rosa Sabatino wanted to rent a place for a pizza parlor. She looked under Rentals and Real Estate. She only found apartments and houses. Then she looked under Business Property. She found a place to rent in a shopping center.

Activity C   Rewrite on your paper the ad below so that someone looking to buy a video game player might find it in the classifieds. In brackets [ ] after the ad, write the section of the classifieds in which you think the ad should be placed.

FOR SALE   Cartridge-type computer player. Almost new, with 10 games. $75. Call 340-9800 and ask for Sue.

Activity D   Use the classified index on page 192. Write the section where you would probably find these products or services listed.

1) People who groom poodles

2) People who lend money

3) A computer training school

4) Help with income taxes

5) People who plan parties

6) A list of jobs

7) A bricklayer

8) Apartments for rent

9) Automobiles for sale

10) Houses for sale

Reading Classified Ads

The price of a classified ad is usually determined by the number of lines in the ad. Abbreviations are often used to keep the ad short and the price down. You will have an easier time finding what you want in the classifieds if you know the meaning of some of these abbreviations.

Abbreviations Used in Housing Advertisements

a/c	—	air conditioned
apt.	—	apartment
BA	—	bathroom
bdrm.	—	bedroom
BR	—	bedroom
carp.	—	carpeting
Condo.	—	Condominium
dep.	—	deposit
Effcy.	—	efficiency
EHO	—	Equal Housing Opportunity
elec.	—	electricity
firepl.	—	fireplace
gar.	—	garage
incl.	—	including
kit.	—	kitchen
MBR	—	master bedroom
NS	—	nonsmoker
Rte.	—	route
shpng.	—	shopping
spac.	—	spacious (large and roomy)
TH	—	townhouse
TV	—	television
utils.	—	utilities
w/d	—	washer and dryer

Activity E   Study the sample apartment ads. Use the information on page 195 to answer the questions that follow. Write your answers on your paper.

GAITH/Ivy Oak   3 BR TH, 1 1/2 BA, covered gar. $800 + elec. 555-900-1092.

GAITH   1 & 2 BR apts. starting at $558, all utils. incl. Call for details, 555-201-2000. EHO.

HYATTS   2 BR, a/c. Pets welcome. $660 incl. utils. 555-188-0910.

HYATTS   Bsmt. apt. for NS. 1 BR. New paint/carp/kit. Walk shpng./buses. Avail 3/1. $395/mo. + dep. + utils. 555-091-8990.

HYATTS   1 & 2 BRs. $450 utils incl. 2 wks free rent. 555-982-0001.

LAUREL   Small cozy community on Rte. 197, 2 bdrms, convenient to Rte. 1. From $540. EHO. Call 555-099-0111.

CONDO   Walking dist. to bus. Effcy. Pool. $570. No pets. Util. incl. 987-320-7400.

WILTON   1 & 2 BR, Newly renovated. With w/d, pool, adults only building. $710 & $875 + elec. 555-420-0910.

---

1) Name three kinds of information contained in every ad.

2) Which apartment has air conditioning?

3) Which apartments include utilities (heat and electricity)? Which apartment owners require that you pay electricity only?

4) Which apartment includes a washer and dryer?

5) Which apartments might you choose if you like to swim?

6) Which apartments would not be good for someone with children?

7) Which apartments might suit someone without a car?

8) Which apartments would not be good for someone with a dog?

9) Which apartment has a parking garage?

10) Which one of these ads is for a townhouse?

Abbreviations Used in Automobile Advertisements

5 spd	—	5-speed transmission
4 dr	—	4 door
6 cyl	—	6 cylinder engine
a/c	—	air conditioning
lo mi	—	low mileage
int	—	interior (refers to upholstery)
inte	—	interior
rear defr	—	rear window defroster
auto	—	automatic transmission
air	—	air conditioned
ps	—	power steering
pb	—	power brakes
pwr	—	power
sunrf	—	sunroof
eng	—	engine
74K	—	74,000 miles
fact. warr.	—	factory warranty
am/fm	—	AM/FM radio
cass	—	cassette tape player
CD	—	compact disc player
conv	—	convertible
pl	—	power locks
4wd	—	four-wheel drive
excl/cond	—	excellent condition
pw	—	power windows

Activity F Study the sample classifieds. Use the information on page 197 to answer the questions that follow. Write your answers on your paper.

AUTOMOBILES—IMPORTS (1455)

AUDI '95 4000S. Auto. 4 dr excel. body & int. Needs eng. work. Best offer. 809-555-1021.

HONDA '94 Civic LX, 4 dr coupe. 5 spd, a/c, stereo, pwr windows & sunrf, low miles. LIKE NEW! Call 703-555-0920.

NISSAN '92—240SX GPL, AC, ster., 5 spd, blue met., $10,995. 901-555-1000.

PORSCHE '96, 944S 11 Cabriolet, triple black. Cruise, pwr. top, airbags, alarm, leather. Loaded. Fact. warr. 1 owner. Car phone. Only 3450 mi. Listed for $51,000. Make offer. Save thousands! 809-555-0102.

AUTOMOBILES—DOMESTIC (1460)

CHEVY '92 GEO Storm, 5 spd, AC, PS, PB, AM/FM stereo cass, 61K mi. Call today for special sale price. JACK'S CHEVROLET. 201-555-9800.

DODGE '93 Dynasty, loaded, fact. warr., lo mi. A steal if you buy today. 890-555-8000. Ask for Sam.

FORD '94 Tempo GL, 4 dr auto a/c ps pb, stereo, rear defr. Today's bargain prices. 800-555-9088.

---

1) Name three kinds of information contained in each ad.

2) Which car has a rear window defroster?

3) Which cars are made by American companies?

4) What does "4 spd" mean?

5) What does "4 dr" mean?

6) Which cars come with a factory warranty?

7) Which cars have air conditioning?

8) What does "auto" mean?

9) Which cars have power steering and power brakes?

10) Write the ad for the Porsche on your paper. Spell out each abbreviated word.

11) Which car has air conditioning and a sunroof?

Part A Use the classified index on page 192. Write the section on your paper where you would probably find these products or services listed.

1) Used cars for sale

2) Used furniture for sale

3) Apartments for rent

4) Houses for sale

5) Business property to rent

Part B Read these ads. Write on your paper your answers to the questions that follow the ads.

RECREATION AND LEISURE	(300)

VACATION in Bermuda! 7 days, 6 nights, air, hotel, meals incl. $1300. Mac's Travel Services, 540-8009.

PETS AND ANIMALS/CATS	(610)

KITTEN Free. 10 wks., F. b&w, short hair, litter-trained. Suzy, 565-9849.

MERCHANDISE	(700)

DIAMOND RING Perf. cond. Cost $500. Make offer, 450-0982. Ask for Ralph.

1) What color is the kitten? Is it a male or a female?

2) Whom can you call about the diamond ring?

3) How much did the diamond ring originally cost?

4) What is the name of the travel agency that is offering the Bermuda vacation?

5) What is included in the price of the Bermuda vacation?

Activity C Write a classified ad for something that you would like to sell. Limit yourself to three or four lines. Use abbreviations to keep your ad short. Write your ad on your paper.

Many people read the help wanted section of the classified ads to find jobs. People who run businesses use this section of the classifieds to advertise job openings.

Sunday, October 25   *The Daily Banner*   G-1

CLASSIFIED ADVERTISING
Employment

EMPLOYMENT SERVICES (901)

JOB RESUME
$15 & UP
Writing/Editing/Typing
While You Wait. 484-6916

CAREER TRAINING (903)

THE MEDIC SCHOOL. Train med. dental asst. 821-5222.

HELP WANTED (905)

ACCOUNTING CLERK Part time. Entry level position, incls. invoicing, filing, accurate typing, 45/50 WPM. Permanent position, 20-25 hrs. per wk. Security area. Call bet. 9 & 1, 298-4706.

HELP WANTED (905)

ADMINISTRATIVE SECY. $25,500 fee paid. This top Co. needs polished sect'l. talents! Good skills and figure aptitude. 837-0778.

AIR COND & Heat Pump Mechanic fully exp. only. Call Frosty Refrig. 747-2024.

AUTO SALESPERSON Sell and make big money on cars and trucks. Salary plus comm. Benefits. 466-1320.

BOOKKEEPER With aptitude for computerized bkkp. Dependable. 675-1118

CASHIER/CLERK Some exp. req'd. All shifts avail. Apply 100 S. Broad bet 9 & 12 noon.

HELP WANTED (905)

CHEF PASTRY 4 yrs. exp. required, knowledge of European pastry pref. Send résumé to Box CS 47822.

CLERICAL If you love to type, my firm needs your skills. Excellent Salary & Benefits. Call Lisa 539-5804.

CLERK TYPIST General office work, 5 days, vic. Smallwood St. 566-5806.

COMPUTER OPERATOR To work part time eves. Must love to type. WP exp. pref. Pleasant atmosphere, free parking. Call 9-5 at 358-TYPE.

Activity A   Use the sample help wanted ads to answer these questions. Write your answers on your paper.

1) Where can you get training as a dental assistant?

2) What kind of job is open at Frosty Refrigeration?

3) Which jobs require or prefer some experience?

4) What number could you call to get your résumé typed?

5) How are job titles organized in the help wanted section?

Understanding Abbreviations in the Help Wanted Ads

Job titles and other information in the help wanted ads are often abbreviated. The same words may be abbreviated in many different ways.

> **EXAMPLE**
> - Admin. Assistant
> - Administrative Assist.
> - Admin. Asst.
>
> An administrative assistant helps an administrator. An administrator is a supervisor or manager of an office or a company.

Activity B   Write on your paper every abbreviation in the following help wanted ads. Beside each abbreviation, write its meaning. Use the words in the list below to help you figure out the meanings of the abbreviations.

ADMIN ASSISTANT   Opp'ty w/CPA firm. Typing 60 wpm, control logs, gen. ofc. exper. req. Résumé to WPR, POB 551, Fairmont.

ADMIN. ASSIST.   Printing co. needs qual. indiv. immed. Good salary & benefits. Respond to POB 456, Wesleyville.

ADMIN. ASST.   Exec. level. Typing & attention to detail req'd. Also Windows 6.1 and Lotus 1-2-3. Excell. sal., benefits. Call Mr. Kim, 560-8000.

---

with	administrative	Post Office Box	assistance
executive	experience	required	individual
excellent	qualified	words per minute	general
company	and	opportunity	immediately
office	salary	Certified Public Accountant	

Words to Know in the Help Wanted Ads

When looking for a job, there are certain terms you should know. Some of these words describe requirements for specific jobs. Many will appear in the want ads. Others may be used during a job interview. Knowing what these words mean will help you determine if you are qualified for the advertised job.

reliable	dependable; workers who do what they are expected to do
experience	the same kind of work that you have done before
executive	a manager, a supervisor, or an administrator
references	people who know about your work and who will recommend you for a job
qualifications	your skills and work experience
permanent	expected to last a long time
temporary	a limited amount of time
full time	a job that requires approximately 40 hours per week, or 8 hours a day for 5 days
part time	a job that requires less than 40 hours per week
benefits	what workers receive in addition to wages, such as health insurance and vacations

Activity C   Use the words from the list to complete these sentences. Write the words on your paper.

1) Ellis Electronics needs a worker for three weeks. This is a _____ position.

2) Rosa Sabatino needs a server who will be at work on time every day. The person must be _____.

3) Rosa wants a server who has worked at a pizza parlor. She wants someone with _____.

4) Rosa will give her workers these _____: full health insurance and a paid vacation.

5) Dan would like a _____ job working evenings and weekends.

Job Titles

The same type of job may have many names. For example, a teacher may be called an instructor or a trainer. Office workers with typing skills have many job titles. They may be called administrative assistants, typists, secretaries, clerk/typists, or word processors.

The way people do their work has changed because of new technology. Job descriptions and titles have also changed. For example, people who type documents today are often called word processors because they use computers and word processing programs. What these workers type has not changed. How they type has.

Activity D   Read these job descriptions. Then write your answers to the questions that follow on your paper.

WORD PROCESSING ASSISTANT Must type 75 WPM minimum and be reliable. Full time, permanent position. Knowledge of word processing helpful but not necessary. Salary depends on experience. Send references with résumé to Wilson, Inc., 4500 Westfield St., Kingsport.

ADMINISTRATIVE ASSISTANT Responsibilities include supervision of a small staff of office workers. Experience with WordPerfect and computer spreadsheet programs required. 60 wpm typing required. Call 240-7598 for appointment.

---

1) What skill does each of these jobs require?

2) Both of these workers will use word processing equipment. Which company will train the worker?

3) Which job requires recommendations from previous employers?

4) Which job would you apply for if you had computer experience?

Activity E Use the information in the help wanted ads below to answer the questions that follow. Write your answers on your paper.

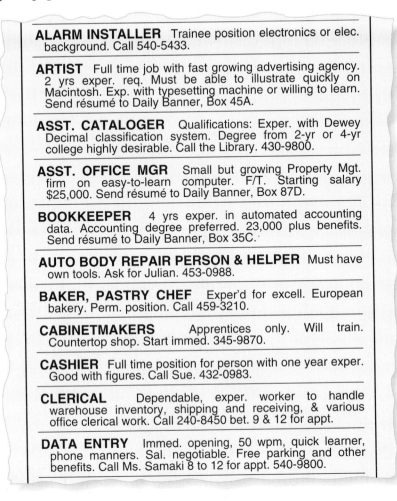

ALARM INSTALLER Trainee position electronics or elec. background. Call 540-5433.

ARTIST Full time job with fast growing advertising agency. 2 yrs exper. req. Must be able to illustrate quickly on Macintosh. Exp. with typesetting machine or willing to learn. Send résumé to Daily Banner, Box 45A.

ASST. CATALOGER Qualifications: Exper. with Dewey Decimal classification system. Degree from 2-yr or 4-yr college highly desirable. Call the Library. 430-9800.

ASST. OFFICE MGR Small but growing Property Mgt. firm on easy-to-learn computer. F/T. Starting salary $25,000. Send résumé to Daily Banner, Box 87D.

BOOKKEEPER 4 yrs exper. in automated accounting data. Accounting degree preferred. 23,000 plus benefits. Send résumé to Daily Banner, Box 35C.

AUTO BODY REPAIR PERSON & HELPER Must have own tools. Ask for Julian. 453-0988.

BAKER, PASTRY CHEF Exper'd for excell. European bakery. Perm. position. Call 459-3210.

CABINETMAKERS Apprentices only. Will train. Countertop shop. Start immed. 345-9870.

CASHIER Full time position for person with one year exper. Good with figures. Call Sue. 432-0983.

CLERICAL Dependable, exper. worker to handle warehouse inventory, shipping and receiving, & various office clerical work. Call 240-8450 bet. 9 & 12 for appt.

DATA ENTRY Immed. opening, 50 wpm, quick learner, phone manners. Sal. negotiable. Free parking and other benefits. Call Ms. Samaki 8 to 12 for appt. 540-9800.

1) Choose four of the positions. List the qualifications required for the jobs.

2) Write the abbreviations that match each of these terms.

    a) full time   **d)** words per minute

    b) permanent   **e)** salary

    c) appointment   **f)** immediately

3) In which jobs will workers receive on-the-job training?

4) Which jobs require education beyond high school?

5) Which jobs will probably cover health care premiums?

Part A Write on your paper the answers to these questions.

1) What word would you look for in the newspaper index to find the help wanted ads?

2) Put these job titles in the order that you would expect to find them in the help wanted ads.

   a) Computer Operator

   b) Machinist

   c) Accountant

3) What does it mean if an ad says that a job is "open"?

4) About how many hours would you expect to work each week in a full time job?

5) Name one of the benefits an employer might offer besides wages.

6) Name one qualification, other than skills and experience, that many employers say they want.

Part B List all of the abbreviations in these ads on your paper. Beside each abbreviation, write the word or words you think the abbreviation stands for.

DATA DISTRIBUTION SPECIALIST Entry level pos. in our mail room. If you have good organizational skills, your own trans., and are able to lift 50 lb., we want to talk to you. Typ. is helpful. Call Mrs. Verney, 450-9800.

BOOKKEEPER/PAYROLL Reliable individual w/exper. working computerized payroll. Needed immed. Good sal. & benefits. Call 321-0984.

CARPET MECHANIC Excellent opp. Must have truck & tools. Apply in person. CarpetTown, 1200 Eastern Avenue, Milton.

BOOK STORE F/T sales/cashier pos. Previous exper. Call 453-0939 for appt.

BEAUTICIAN F/T or P/T. Exp. pref. Start immed. Call Joy. 432-4900.

Television and radio communications have changed the way we get information about the world. Instead of reading about important events in the newspaper after they occur, we see these events or hear about them *as they happen.*

Broadcast

To send radio or television signals through the air to receivers in the home, the car, or other location.

Television and radio stations **broadcast**, or send, signals through the air to receivers in the home, the car, or wherever we are. Signals also come to us from communications satellites orbiting around the earth, microwave transmitters, and telephone lines. They also come into our homes through cables and satellite dishes.

Broadcast television is free to anyone who has a television set and an antenna. To receive information using other methods, people purchase or rent a telephone, cable box, or satellite dish. They also pay a monthly fee.

Cable television has increased the number of television channels from a few to more than 100. More than 65 percent of people have cable TV and the percentage is increasing each year.

Many people also use their television sets to watch movies on videocassettes or videodiscs. Some people use them to play video games.

Radio, too, plays a major role in people's lives. People listen to radio for music, news, weather, and traffic reports. People call in and discuss their opinions or ask questions on talk radio programs, which are very popular. People with Citizens Band (CB) receivers in their cars and homes may talk to people all over the world using radio signals.

Activity A Write on your paper your answers to these questions.

1) Name four ways that television and radio signals can reach our receivers.

2) Name at least two ways that people use television other than for watching TV programs.

3) What does CB stand for?

Television Literacy

TV viewing plays an important part in our lives. In the United States, 99% of the households have at least one color television set. If you want to use TV as an information tool, you need to understand the television industry. The goal of the next few activities is to help you become "television literate."

Did you know?

- A recent survey shows that in the average American home, a television set is on about 7 hours per day. That is nearly 30% of the 168 hours in one week.

- Women who are 18 to 24 years old watch, on average, about 4 hours more per week than men of the same age group. Throughout their lives, women watch more television than men, on average.

- On the average, male and female teenagers watch television over 20 hours per week.

- America's favorite shows are comedies, dramatic series, football games, and movies. Americans especially enjoy the Super Bowl—an annual football game that determines the year's champion football team. In fact, the 50 most popular television shows from 1964 to 1994 included 18 Super Bowl games.

USING WHAT YOU HAVE LEARNED

Survey your class to find out if your group has the same tastes as average American viewers. Have each person list his or her five favorite TV programs. Beside each person's name, write the types of programs that person has listed: comedy, drama, sports, movies, news. (If your classmates are like most American viewers, their favorite programs will be situation comedies.)

Television Viewing and Advertising

Much of what we see on television is commercial advertising. Audience viewing habits are important to the TV industry and especially to companies that advertise on television. Obviously, the more people who see an advertisement the better.

Who cares how much TV certain people watch and what shows people like best?

Advertisers and television station owners care very much. TV programs and commercials are expensive to make. Advertisers pay high fees to have them broadcast. They want the largest audiences possible.

How much money do TV advertisers spend each year?

Advertisers spend more than 23 billion dollars each year advertising on television. That includes the amount they spend on network TV, syndicated TV, and cable TV. Businesses spend such large amounts of money because television stations promise that a certain number of people will be watching.

How do advertisers know which programs are popular? How do they know what kinds of people are watching?

The Nielsen Company reports on how many people watch each program. They choose about 1,200 families to represent the population. The families include young, old, rich, poor, and "average" people. The Nielsen sample is a small part of the entire TV viewing population.

Advertisers and TV stations are interested in what programs people watch during prime time. When is prime time?

Prime time

The hours when television is watched the most, between 8 P.M. and 11 P.M.

Prime time is between 8 P.M. and 11 P.M. each day (7 P.M. and 10 P.M. in some time zones). TV has its largest audience during these hours. TV stations charge the most for ads shown during those hours.

TV advertisers try to find out whether the viewing audience is made up of mostly men or women. They want to know as much as possible about those people. Then they advertise their products on shows with a certain kind of audience.

Activity B   Write on your paper your answer to the following question. Then share and discuss your answer with the class.

How much do advertisements that you see on television affect what products you buy?

Activity C   Write on your paper the kinds of products you would expect to be advertised on a show that is aimed at each of the following audiences. Then compare and discuss your answers with your class.

1) Mostly teenagers

2) Mostly men

3) Mostly women

4) Mostly children

5) Mostly older people (over 50)

6) Professionals and business people

Advertisers know that teens watch sporting events. Many products teens use are advertised on TV during these events.

Kinds of TV Stations

- **Network television**

  A network is a large TV corporation that has member stations. It broadcasts its signal over the airways to these member stations all over the United States. Four of the largest TV networks are American Broadcasting Company (ABC), Columbia Broadcasting System (CBS), National Broadcasting Company (NBC), and Fox Broadcasting Company. Each network earns money by selling airtime to advertisers. The member stations are called **affiliates**. Each affiliate carries some of the network programming and other local programming. Affiliates provide local news, weather, sports, and other shows directed at a small portion of the country. Affiliates sell airtime to local advertisers.

- **Independent stations**

  This group of small TV companies may own one or several stations. Independent stations also sell advertising time. They may produce some original programs, but they usually buy programs from syndicates. Many independent stations broadcast old movies, game shows, and reruns of shows first shown on network stations.

- **Public Broadcasting System (PBS)**

  This network of educational television stations does not accept advertisements. PBS stations get much of their money from people who watch the station and send in **donations**. A donation is a gift of money or other items of value. Businesses also donate money as a public service. The federal government and some state governments also give money to public television stations. These stations offer college courses, documentaries, news, entertainment programming, and children's programming.

- **Cable networks**

  These corporations send program signals by cable or satellite dish to local cable companies. The local cable company sells these programs to its customers, or **subscribers**, by providing what is called cable service. There are many cable networks.

Affiliate

A member station that carries some of the programs broadcast by a large television network.

Donation

A gift of money or other items of value.

Subscriber

A customer of a local cable television company.

Some of the most popular are the Cable News Network (CNN); the Discovery Channel; USA Network; Music Television Network (MTV); Turner Broadcasting System (TBS); Black Entertainment Television (BET); The Nashville Network (TNN); and ESPN. All of these cable networks have millions of subscribers. Most cable networks focus on one main type of programming. For example, ESPN presents sports programming; CNN is all news; and MTV has music videos. These networks sell advertising time. Advertisers and subscription fees pay for the programming.

- **Premium cable networks and pay-per-view TV**
These networks do not have advertisements. Subscribers pay extra fees that cover the cost of this programming. Home Box Office (HBO), Showtime, Cinemax, The Disney Channel, and The Movie Channel are some of the main premium networks. These stations show mainly movies. Sometimes these channels have special features and other types of programming. On pay-per-view TV channels, people call the local cable company and order programs. They pay a fee for each program they request. Pay-per-view TV offers current movies and special sports programming.

- **Syndicates**
A syndicate is a company or organization that sells television programs to television stations. The syndicate buys the programming from other producers. Game shows and talk shows are popular syndicated programs. You will see these programs on different channels in different cities. Syndicates also purchase old network programs and sell them to independent and local stations.

Activity D   Look at the example of part of the daily television broadcast schedule in the newspaper for one city. Then answer on your paper the questions that follow.

		NBC **4** WRC	FOX **5** WTTG	ABC **7** WJLA	CBS **9** WUSA	**20** WDCA	**50** WBDC
6	:00	NBC News	News	ABC News	News	K. Copeland	Movie (cont.)
	:30	News	News	News		Jetsons	Heathcliff
7	:00	Today	Fox Morning News	Good Morning America	This Morning	Flintstones	Felix the Cat
	:30					Wake, Rattle	Video Power

1) What are four of the largest network channels?

2) Name the independent channels.

3) What does each independent channel broadcast at 7:30?

4) Name the call letters for Channel 5.

5) What major network is Channel 5 an affiliate of?

The newspaper schedule does not list every station that viewers in that area can watch. A TV program guide on sale at newsstands has a more complete listing. Below is a listing for one time slot on a certain evening.

11:30 P.M.		
2 **4**	TONIGHT	Host: Jay Leno
5	PERSONALITIES	
7 **45**	NIGHTLINE	
9	LATE SHOW WITH DAVID LETTERMAN	
11	EVENING SHADE	
20	STAR TREK: THE NEXT GENERATION	
26	CHARLIE ROSE	
32	ITN WORLD NEWS	
50	DESIGNING WOMEN	

Activity E   Use the information in both programming guides on page 212 to answer the questions. Write your answers on your paper.

1) On which two channels is *Nightline* broadcast at 11:30 P.M.?

2) Name the program that WTTG will show at 11:30 P.M.

3) What program does channel 50 show at 11:30 P.M.?

4) Who is the host of *The Tonight Show*?

5) On which network does David Letterman appear?

6) What program does WDCA show at 11:30 P.M.?

Activity F   Use the information on pages 210–212 to answer these questions. Write your answers on your paper.

1) What type of programming does each of the following cable stations show?

  a) ESPN

  b) CNN

  c) MTV

2) Name three kinds of programs that PBS stations offer.

3) What television network operates WUSA, Channel 9?

4) What program does WJLA show at 7 A.M. every weekday morning?

5) Which station could you tune in to see a movie at 6 A.M.?

6) How many stations are broadcasting news at 7 A.M.?

Educational TV Stations

Today, many stations besides PBS broadcast educational programs. Here are some subjects you may find on these channels:

EXAMPLES	
Computer education	How to buy life insurance
Managing a business	How to invest your money
How to find a job	Sewing, cooking, and gardening

Educational channels and PBS stations also have news programming that focuses on the government and the stock market. Some programs are about historical events. They are called **documentaries**. A documentary is a nonfiction film.

Documentary

A nonfiction film or television program.

Radio Broadcasting

Each radio station usually has a special type of programming, such as all news, rock and roll, or classical music.

You may like to explore the different stations on your radio. Although radio stations also belong to networks, their programs are different in each area. You can usually find more local news on the radio than on TV. Radio is also one of the most up-to-the-minute sources of news.

The Federal Communications Commission

Federal Communications Commission (FCC)

A government agency that provides licenses to people or companies to operate television and radio stations.

The **Federal Communications Commission (FCC)** is a government agency that gives licenses to people or companies that want to operate television and radio stations. The FCC also makes rules for these stations. The rules indicate how much air time stations can sell to commercial advertisers.

Radio and TV stations broadcast their signals over the air. The airways belong to the public, which is why the government controls their use. Each station must broadcast over a specific frequency. Citizens Band (CB) radio also has a certain frequency. The word *band* means a certain range of frequencies.

Lesson Review   Write on your paper the answers to these questions.

1) What are two ways that radio and television signals are sent?

2) What is the name of the federal agency that makes rules for radio and television stations?

3) What do the initials "CB" mean?

4) Approximately how many hours a week is a television set on in the average American household?

5) How do the owners of TV stations and TV networks earn money?

6) Which TV viewing hours are called "prime time"?

7) Why do TV station owners charge more money to show a commercial during prime time?

8) What are the four major TV networks?

9) What do the initials "PBS" mean?

10) What are two ways that PBS stations receive money?

11) What are stations called that do not belong to a network?

12) What is a documentary?

13) How are pay-per-view TV stations different from network stations?

14) What does the Nielsen Rating Service do for the TV networks?

Chapter 7 Review

Part A Write the best answer for each question on your paper.

1) Which are mass media?

   a) newspapers

   b) letters

   c) telephone calls

2) Which of these media has the most facts about job openings?

   a) television

   b) radio

   c) newspaper

3) Which section of a newspaper has opinions about current events?

   a) front page

   b) classified

   c) editorial

4) Who decides which stories to print and how long they will be—the reporter or the editor?

5) Which TV network has educational programming without commercial advertising—HBO, PBS, or NBC?

Part B Write on your paper your answers to these questions.

1) What six questions should a news story answer?

2) What are four parts, or sections, of a newspaper?

3) What is an example of an advertising slogan?

4) What are the initials of the federal agency that makes rules for radio and TV stations.

5) What does the term *documentary* mean?

Part C   Write on your paper all of the abbreviations in these ads. Beside each abbreviation, write its meaning.

JACKSON HEIGHTS   2 BR apt., A/C, 5 min. walk to bus. $675 + elec. 246-9871

CHEVETTE   91, 4 dr., 4 cyl., ps, pb, red w/white int. Best offer. 235-7109.

CLERK   F/T, 50 wpm, exper. req. Sal. $18,000 to start. Send résumé to Daily Banner, POB 34D.

Test Taking Tip   Look over a test before you begin answering questions. See how many parts there are. See what you are being asked to do on each part.

Chapter

8

Completing Applications and Other Forms

Throughout your life, you will be asked to fill out forms. You may have to fill out a form to apply for a job, to obtain a driver's license, to rent an apartment, to open a checking account, or to travel to another country. A form is a printed or typed document with spaces to fill in information about you or someone else.

In Chapter 8, you will learn about completing different types of applications and forms. Each lesson focuses on the kinds of information you have to know to fill out forms and the different kinds of forms you may have to fill out.

Goals for Learning

▶ To learn how to fill out applications and other forms correctly and completely

▶ To learn about the kinds of personal information asked for on applications and forms

▶ To learn how to answer questions on job applications

▶ To learn about questions and vocabulary related to loans, credit, and financial forms

Document
A paper that gives information to another person.

Form
A printed or typed document with spaces to fill in information.

Full name
A person's whole legal name.

Maiden name
A woman's last name before she marries.

Personal information
Facts about yourself.

Signature
The name of a person written by that person.

Almost every **form** you complete asks for **personal information**. Personal information includes facts about yourself. You should know your Social Security number, date and place of birth, and telephone number. Sometimes you will be asked for the full names of your parents. You may also be asked for your mother's **maiden name**. A woman's maiden name is her last name before she marries and takes her husband's last name. Women are not required to take a husband's last name, but many women do. You may also be asked for the names and ages of your brothers and sisters.

It is important to know your **full name**, or your legal name.

Most forms must be signed with a legal **signature**. A signature is a person's name written by that person. You will use your legal signature on legal papers such as checks and other **documents**. A document is a paper that gives information to another person. You must always write, not print, your legal signature. You may also use your initials.

On most forms, you will need to provide your complete mailing address. Depending on the form, you may or may not be able to use abbreviations, or short forms of words. You will probably need to know the two-letter postal abbreviation for your state.

Activity A   Write on your paper these facts about yourself.

1) Your Social Security number

2) Your date of birth (month, day, year)

3) Your place of birth (city, state, country)

4) Your home telephone number, including area code

5) Your father's full name

6) Your mother's full name

7) Your mother's maiden name

8) The names and ages of your brothers and sisters

Activity B Write on your paper the answers to these questions about yourself.

1) What is your full, legal name? Include your middle name if you have one.

2) Write your legal signature. Do not print your signature.

3) What is your complete address? Do not use any abbreviations. Use capitals and punctuation correctly. Follow the example below:

Mr. Howard Simmons
2121 48th Avenue, Apartment 101A
Seat Pleasant, Maryland 20716

4) What is the two-letter postal abbreviation of the state in which you live? For example, the abbreviation for California is CA.

5) What is your Social Security number?

6) What is your telephone number with the area code? Use this format: (301) 555-2938.

Your Name and Your Signature

You probably do not use your full, legal name all the time. People with nicknames, such as Rob for Roberto or Pam for Pamela, often sign their names that way. However, if you buy a house or rent an apartment, you will usually sign your full, legal name. When you open a checking account at a bank, you fill out a signature card. You are to sign your name on your checks exactly as you write it on that card.

Ray D. Ryan

Anna Maria DeMarco

Andy Thomas

Leon Jones-Washington

Your Address

Most forms ask for your mailing address. Be sure that you can write your address in the correct form.

> **EXAMPLE**
>
> Mrs. Anna M. Wong
> 13 West Park Avenue
> Apt. 102
> Seattle, WA 98109

Postal Codes

The post office has its own method of abbreviating state names. The U.S. Postal Service uses a two-letter postal code. Both letters are capitalized and no periods are used. These abbreviations are used when you write addresses. In other situations, write out the full name of the state.

Activity C Write each of these state abbreviations on your paper. Next to the abbreviation, write the name of the state in full. Use a dictionary if necessary.

1) AK	11) HI	21) ME	31) NJ	41) SD
2) AL	12) IA	22) MI	32) NM	42) TN
3) AR	13) ID	23) MN	33) NV	43) TX
4) AZ	14) IL	24) MS	34) NY	44) UT
5) CA	15) IN	25) MO	35) OH	45) VA
6) CO	16) KS	26) MT	36) OK	46) VT
7) CT	17) KY	27) NC	37) OR	47) WA
8) DE	18) LA	28) ND	38) PA	48) WI
9) FL	19) MA	29) NE	39) RI	49) WV
10) GA	20) MD	30) NH	40) SC	50) WY

Your Social Security Number

Almost every form and application you will ever fill out will ask for your Social Security number. For example:

- A bank, when you open a savings account.

- Your employer, when you apply for a job.

- The government, when you file a tax return.

- A stockbroker, if you buy stocks or bonds.

- Colleges, if you enroll in courses.

- The Social Security Administration, if you apply for benefits.

When you apply for a Social Security card, the form asks for your full name as used in business and for the names of your parents.

Activity D   In your own words, explain in one or two sentences why it is important to have a Social Security card. Write your explanation on your paper.

You must fill out an application to receive a Social Security card.

Your Birth Certificate

To apply for a Social Security number, you will need an official copy of your birth certificate. An official copy of a birth certificate has a raised seal. A photocopy is not acceptable. If you don't have a copy, contact the capital of the state where you were born. Give them your full name and date of birth and ask them to send you your birth certificate. You will probably have to pay a fee.

If you were born in the United States, you are a United States citizen. If you were born in another country and one of your parents is a U.S. citizen, you are also a U.S. citizen.

A person who was not born in the United States may apply for citizenship. He or she then becomes a "naturalized" citizen and receives citizenship papers. These people have all of the rights and responsibilities of native citizens.

A person who was not born in the United States and who is not a naturalized citizen must register with the state as an alien. He or she may then apply for a green card. A green card is an official document that allows aliens to work legally in the United States. Green cards used to be the color green. They are still called green cards even though they are no longer that color.

Activity E   Write on your paper your answers to these questions. Then discuss your answers with your class.

1) When might it be important to have a birth certificate that proves you were born in the United States?

2) When might you have to use your birth certificate to prove your age?

3) What does someone who is not a citizen need to work legally in the United States?

4) What city and state would you contact to get a copy of your birth certificate?

Part A   Number your paper from 1 to 9. Write the correct letter of the definition beside the number of each word.

Terms

1) Form

2) Document

3) Social Security number

4) Signature

5) Birth certificate

6) Citizen

7) Legal name

8) Maiden name

9) Telephone number

Meanings

a) A printed paper with spaces to fill in information

b) 214-45-4501

c) A woman's last name at birth

d) Name recorded at birth

e) (931) 264-4592

f) Your name as you write it

g) Person belonging to a country

h) Official paper stating when and where a person was born

i) A paper with official information

Part B   Write on your paper your answers to these questions.

1) What is your legal name?

2) What is your signature?

3) What is your mother's maiden name?

4) What is your Social Security number?

5) What do you need to know and what documents do you need when you apply for a Social Security number?

Part C   Write this mailing address on your paper. Put the information in the correct order and spell it correctly.

Ms. Tara Gillan, Franklin, Pa 15222, Route 1, P.O. Box 23

You will often have to complete an **application** form. An application is a form to make a request. A job application form is your request that a company consider you for a job. You will have to provide many kinds of information on application forms.

Here is a list of words you will find on many job application forms.

Words	Meanings
Position	The name of your job
Employer	The person or company that pays you a salary
Employee	A person who works for someone else
Supervisor	Your boss
Salary	Amount of money you are paid
Previous/Former	Something that happened in the past
Available	When you can begin a job

Here is part of a job application form.

Employer _____

Address _____

Phone (___) _____

Supervisor _____

Dates employed: from ___/___/___ to ___/___/___

Position title _____

No. hours worked/week _____

Salary: starting $_____ ☐ hourly ☐ weekly ☐ monthly

ending $_____ ☐ hourly ☐ weekly ☐ monthly

Description of work: _____

_____

_____

_____

Application
A form to make a request.

Available
Refers to when you can begin a job.

Employee
A person who works for someone else.

Employer
A person or company that pays you a salary.

Former
Refers to something that happened in the past.

Position
The name of your job.

Previous
Refers to something that happened in the past.

Salary
The amount of money you are paid for working.

Supervisor
A person who is your boss.

Advice for Completing Applications

Rule 1   Answer every question. Never leave a question unanswered. The employer will think you forgot to answer it or that you cannot answer it.

Rule 2   There may be some questions that are not **applicable** to you. Applicable means suitable or appropriate. You do not have to answer questions that are not applicable. Instead, you can write N/A for not applicable in those spaces. The employer will know that you read the question.

Rule 3   Always print or type your answers. Often people do not get a job because the employer can't read their application form.

Rule 4   Be sure your answers are correct. Every fact on your application must be accurate. If the employer tries to call you to offer you the job, you want the right phone number on your application. At the end of the form, you will be asked to sign it to verify that all the information is true and accurate. Any false answer that you provide could mean that you will not get the job.

Activity A   Answer the following questions.

1) Some employers "grade" a job application. They check the answer to every question and give the application a score. The people with the highest scores are then interviewed. What do you think a neat, complete, and correct job application tells the employer about you?

2) Why should you be very careful that your answers are correct?

3) What is the difference between a "false" answer and a mistake? Is there any way for an employer to know why the information is wrong?

Questions About Your Education

Education

A combination of the courses and programs taken at a school or college.

Whenever you apply for a job, you will be asked about your **education**. Education refers to the courses and programs you have taken at any school or college.

Keep your educational records in a special place. You may change jobs several times during your career. Each time you apply for a new job, you will need this information.

Here is a sample of a completed job application form. Notice how many items relate to education.

Job Application Form

Print Name _Margaret Louisa Gomez_

Address _9301 Watkins Ave., Apt. 101, Wilton, Delaware 19973_

Home Phone _(302) 217-3881_ Business Phone _(302) 217-2800_

College or University: _University of Delaware, Newark, Delaware_

Major and specialty: _Business Administration, Accounting_

Dates attended: From _9/85_ To _6/89_   Degree received ☑Yes ☐ No

If yes, give title and date _B.S. 6/89_

If no, give number of credit hours completed _N/A_ Years completed: _N/A_

List pertinent courses completed _Accounting, Marketing,_

Business Administration

Other Training: _Wilton Business School, Wilton, Delaware_
                     (Name and Location of School)

Subject studied: _Word Processing, Computerized Bookkeeping_

Dates attended: From _9/92_ To _6/94_   Years completed: Day ___ Night _2_

Activity B   Answer these questions about yourself. Print your answers on your paper.

1) What was the name of the last high school you attended?

2) Where was this school located (city and state)?

3) When did you attend this school (From _____ To _____)?

4) On what date did you graduate or do you expect to graduate?

5) What were the chief courses that you took?

Your Job Skills

Employers want to know about your skills. When you apply for a job, list skills that are **pertinent**. That means the skills that are applicable to the job for which you are applying. Here are some machines that office workers often use. A person applying for an office job might list all or some of these on an application.

Pertinent

Applicable.

- copier
- word processor
- document binder
- FAX machine
- telephones
- calculator
- dictation machine
- switchboard
- computer
- printers
- videotape recorders and camcorders
- audiocassette players and recorders
- postage meter

Activity C Answer these questions about yourself. Print your answers on your paper.

1) List any machines that you can operate. Describe in your own words why you think being able to operate a specific machine will help you get the job you want.

2) Can you type? If yes, give the number of words per minute (wpm). Do you think knowing how to type is a useful skill? Explain your answer.

3) Can you use a computer? What kinds of computer systems have you used?

4) Have you ever used a computer for schoolwork? If yes, describe when. Have you ever used a computer on a volunteer or paid job? If yes, describe when.

5) What kinds of software can you use? Examples are word processing, spreadsheet, database management, accounting, graphics, and desktop publishing.

6) List any other special skills that you have.

If you apply for a data entry job, you should list all of your computer skills.

Activity D   Use the information in the sample job application form on page 228 to answer these questions. Write your answers on your paper.

1) Name the college that Margaret Louisa Gomez attended.

2) What was her major course of study?

3) Did she graduate from college? If so, when?

4) What kind of degree did she earn?

5) Which of her college courses did Margaret think were pertinent to this job?

6) What does N/A mean?

7) What other school did Margaret attend?

8) Did Margaret take any computer courses? If yes, what kind?

Questions About Your Employer and Immediate Supervisor

Your employer is the person or company that you work for. Your immediate supervisor is your boss, the person who tells you what to do. Your employer and your immediate supervisor can be the same person; however, they usually are different people.

> **EXAMPLES**   Joseph Piña works for Howard J. Dauss, Contractors. Mr. Dauss owns the company. He pays Joseph for his work. Mr. Dauss is Joseph's employer.
>
> Joseph is an apprentice plumber for the company. His boss is a foreman. The foreman's name is Mike Sievers. Mike is Joseph's immediate supervisor.

Questions About Your Positions and Job Titles

A position is a job title. It is the name of a job. By knowing job titles, you can find jobs that interest you in the help wanted ads in the newspaper.

EXAMPLES

apprentice plumber
bookkeeper
carpenter
computer technician
electrician journeyman
layout drafter
leasing agent
receptionist
secretary
senior bus driver

Activity E   Use the information above and on page 231 to answer these questions. Write your answers on your paper.

1) What is Joseph Piña's job title?

2) Who is Joseph Piña's immediate supervisor?

3) Who is Joseph Piña's employer?

4) On your own paper, make a chart of your employment history. Start with the most recent job and work back. List every job, including part-time, temporary, or volunteer positions. Use these headings to create your chart: *Dates of Employment, Position, Employer, Supervisor.*

DATES OF EMPLOYMENT	POSITION	EMPLOYER	SUPERVISOR

More About Your Work Experience

The Standard Form 171 is the name of the federal government job application form. It is also called a Personal Qualifications Statement. It is a good example of the information you need to know about your experience.

WORK EXPERIENCE *If you have no work experience, write "NONE" and go to 25 on page 3.*

23 May we ask your present employer about your character, qualifications, and work record? *A "NO" will not affect our review of your qualifications. If you answer "NO" and we need to contact your present employer before we can offer you a job, we will contact you first.* . . . . | YES | NO |

24 READ **WORK EXPERIENCE** IN THE INSTRUCTIONS BEFORE YOU BEGIN.

- Describe your current or most recent job in Block **A** and work backwards, describing each job you held **during the past 10 years**. If you were **unemployed** for longer than **3 months** within the past 10 years, list the dates and your address(es) in an experience block.
- You may sum up in one block work that you did **more than 10 years ago**. But if that work **is related** to the type of job you are applying for, describe each related job in a separate block.
- INCLUDE VOLUNTEER WORK *(non-paid work)*--**If the work** (or a part of the work) **is like the job you are applying for,** complete **all** parts of the experience block just as you would for a paying job. You may receive credit for work experience with religious, community, welfare, service, and other organizations.

- INCLUDE MILITARY SERVICE--You should complete **all** parts of the experience block just as you would for a non-military job, including all supervisory experience. Describe each major change of duties or responsibilities in a separate experience block.
- IF YOU NEED MORE SPACE TO DESCRIBE A JOB--Use sheets of paper the same size as this page (be sure to include **all** information we ask for in **A** and **B** below). On **each** sheet show your name, Social Security Number, and the announcement number or job title.
- IF YOU NEED MORE EXPERIENCE BLOCKS, use the SF 171-A or a sheet of paper.
- IF YOU NEED TO UPDATE (ADD MORE RECENT JOBS), use the SF 172 or a sheet of paper as described above.

A | Name and address of employer's organization *(include ZIP Code, if known)* | Dates employed *(give month, day and year)* | | Average number of hours per week | Number of employees you supervise |
|---|---|---|---|---|
| | From: To: | | | |
| | Salary or earnings
Starting $ per
Ending $ per | | Your reason for wanting to leave | |
| Your immediate supervisor
Name   Area Code   Telephone No. | Exact title of your job | | If Federal employment *(civilian or military)* list series, grade or rank and, if promoted in this job, the date of your last promotion | |

Description of work: Describe your specific duties, responsibilities and accomplishments in this job, **including** the job title(s) of any employees you supervise. *If you describe more than one type of work (for example, carpentry and painting, or personnel and budget), write the approximate percentage of time you spent doing each.*

For Agency Use (skill codes, etc.)

B | Name and address of employer's organization *(include ZIP Code, if known)* | Dates employed *(give month, day and year)* | | Average number of hours per week | Number of employees you supervised |
|---|---|---|---|---|
| | From: To: | | | |
| | Salary or earnings
Starting $ per
Ending $ per | | Your reason for leaving | |
| Your immediate supervisor
Name   Area Code   Telephone No. | Exact title of your job | | If Federal employment *(civilian or military)* list series, grade or rank and, if promoted in this job, the date of your last promotion | |

Description of work: Describe your specific duties, responsibilities and accomplishments in this job, **including** the job title(s) of any employees you supervised. *If you describe more than one type of work (for example, carpentry and painting, or personnel and budget), write the approximate percentage of time you spent doing each.*

For Agency Use (skill codes, etc.)

Page 2 IF YOU NEED MORE EXPERIENCE BLOCKS, USE SF 171-A *(SEE BACK OF INSTRUCTION PAGE).*

Activity F Here are items you would have to fill in on a Standard Form 171. Use a job you have now or one you have had in the past to complete each item. Write your responses on your paper.

1) Name, address, and phone number of employer's organization (include ZIP code and area code)

2) Dates employed (give month, day, and year)
From _____
To _____

3) Average number of hours per week

4) Salary or earnings; $ _____ per week or per hour

5) Place of employment (city and state)

6) Exact title of your position

7) Name of immediate supervisor and phone number (include area code)

8) Number and kind of employees you supervise

9) Kind of business or organization (manufacturing, accounting, social services, etc.)

10) If you worked for the federal government, give your civilian or military series, your grade or rank, and date of last promotion

11) Your reason for wanting to leave

12) Description of work (tell about your specific duties, responsibilities, and accomplishments in this job)

13) Whether your present or former employer can be contacted

Your Job Application References

When you fill out a job application, you are asking that you be hired for a certain job. A reference is a person who will recommend you for that job. Always ask a person's permission before you use his or her name as a reference.

A reference should be

- a person who knows about your skills and past work experience.

- a person who likes and admires you and will say positive things about you.

- a person whom the new employer will believe and respect.

A reference should not be

- a relative.

- a person who did not like you or your work.

USING WHAT YOU HAVE LEARNED

Write the names, complete addresses, and phone numbers in your personal address book of the three people you added to the list in Activity G. You will need this information when you apply for jobs.

Activity G   Explain why each of these people would or would not be a good reference. Write your answers on your paper. Then name three references of your own and explain why each person would be a good reference.

1) A teacher

2) A guidance counselor

3) A previous employer

4) Your present employer

5) Your best friend

6) A relative

7) A member of the clergy

8) Your next-door neighbor

Part A   Write the answers to these questions on your paper.

1) What is the purpose of a job application?

2) What do you write in a space if the question does not apply to you?

3) Why is it important to answer every question on a job application form?

4) You may print or type your answers on a job application. What is the one thing that you must write?

5) What information do you need about people you want to give as references?

6) When you tell about your work experience, which job do you describe first?

Part B   Match the words with their meanings. Write the correct letter next to each number on your paper.

Words

1) Job application
2) Education
3) Reference
4) Work experience
5) Position
6) Immediate supervisor
7) Employer
8) Salary
9) Signature
10) Full name

Meanings

a) Your school experience

b) The name of your job

c) Your boss

d) The person or company you work for

e) A form you fill out to ask for a job

f) Your earnings

g) Your written legal name

h) A person who will recommend you for a job

i) Your first, middle, and last name

j) The jobs you have had

Assets
Property you own that has value.

Debt
Money owed, or liability.

Financial
Concerning money or property with value.

Liability
The money you owe.

Net worth
The value of your assets minus the value of your liabilities.

Value
The amount of money your property is worth to a buyer.

When you borrow money or receive credit, you will be asked questions about your finances. You may need to fill out a **financial** form. Financial matters have to do with money or property with **value**.

You may need to prepare a financial statement at some time. To do this, you will need to list your **liabilities**. A liability is the money you owe to someone. **Debt** is another word for liability or money owed. Then you add up all your **assets** and all your liabilities. The value of your assets minus the value of your liabilities is your **net worth**.

Activity A   Use the sample financial statement to answer the questions below. Write your answers on your paper.

Robert Thompson's Financial Statement

Assets	Liabilities
Car $2,800.00	Car loan at bank $2,300.00
Watch...........................$25.00	Department store credit card $144.32
Stereo $200.00	
Total $3,025.00	**Total $2,444.32**

$3,025.00 Assets
− $2,444.32 Liabilities
$ 580.68 Net worth

1) Which of these two items is an asset?

   a) Things you own with value

   b) Money that you owe

2) List Robert Thompson's assets.

3) How much money does he owe?

4) If Robert sold everything he owns and paid all his debts, how much cash would he have?

Activity B Follow the directions below to prepare a financial statement of your own.

1) Make a list of your assets. Guess what their value is.

2) Make a list of your liabilities (debts).

3) Add up both columns.

4) Subtract your liabilities from your assets.

5) Circle your net worth.

Borrowing Money for a Car or House

Loan

A sum of money that you borrow.

Someday you may wish to obtain a **loan** to buy a car or a house. A loan is a sum of money you borrow. Lenders, or the people who loan money, want to be sure they can get their money back. They will want answers to these questions:

1. How much money can you pay each month? Each month you pay back part of the loan. The bank will ask you about your income and about your other expenses.

2. What is the value of your car or house? You may not be able to make your payments. The bank can sell the car or house to get the money back.

Activity C Write on your paper the answers to these questions.

1) What are two reasons you may wish to get a loan?

2) Why will a lender ask you about your income and other expenses?

3) Why is it important for a lender to know the value of the item you wish to purchase?

4) If you bought a car, how would you list it on your financial statement?

5) How would you list a loan for a car on your financial statement?

6) What do you call the amount of money your car is worth to a buyer?

Credit and Finance Charges

Credit
The time you get to pay for the goods you buy.

Finance charge
A fee you pay on money you owe to a business.

Joint
An account that is shared or owned together.

Merchandise
Goods for sale or that you buy.

Credit is the time you get to pay for goods you buy. The goods you buy are also known as **merchandise**.

Department stores offer credit cards that customers can use to purchase merchandise on credit. If you charge goods on a credit card, the store will send you a monthly bill, or statement. If you pay all of the money you owe on time, you do not have to pay any extra fees. When you pay only a part of what you owe, the store charges you a **finance charge**. A finance charge is the fee you pay for borrowing on credit from a store.

Charge accounts can be individual or **joint.** An individual account means that one person can use the card. A joint account means that two people can use the card. They are both responsible for paying the bill.

Activity D   Here are some of the questions a store may ask you when you apply for a credit card. Answer as many of them as you can. Write your answers on your paper.

1) Will this be an individual or a joint account?

2) What is the name of the applicant (the person applying for the charge card)?

3) What is your Social Security number?

4) What is your date of birth?

5) What is your present address?

6) How long have you been at this address?

7) If you have been at the above address for less than four years, list your former address.

8) What is your phone number? (Include area code.)

9) Who is your current employer?

10) What is your employer's address?

11) What is your business telephone number?

12) What type of business is this?

13) What is your present position?

14) What is your monthly salary?

Bank Accounts

When you ask for a loan or credit, you usually have to provide information about your bank accounts. There are several kinds of bank accounts.

Checking Accounts

You open a checking account by putting some money into the bank. The bank gives you a checkbook. You withdraw money from your account by writing checks. You can write checks to other people or to yourself. You can't write checks for more money than you have in your account. A **deposit** is money you have put into an account.

Deposit
The money you put into an account.

Savings Accounts

You open a savings account by depositing money into the bank. The purpose is to save money. You should not need this money right away. The bank pays you **interest** on this money. Interest is the money a bank pays you for putting money into a savings account. You don't write checks to get your money from a savings account; you use a **withdrawal** slip. A withdrawal is the money you have taken from your account.

Interest
The money a bank pays you for putting money into a savings account; the fee you pay for borrowing money.

Loan Accounts

You open a loan account when you borrow money. Every month you make a payment to pay back part of the loan. Included in your monthly payment is interest. The interest on a loan is the fee you pay to the bank or lender for borrowing money.

Withdrawal
Money that you have taken out of your bank account.

Activity E   Write on your paper your answers to these questions about bank accounts.

1) Name three kinds of bank accounts.

2) Which type of bank account pays you interest?

3) On which account do you pay interest?

4) How do you add money to your checking account balance?

5) How do you withdraw money from a checking account?

6) Which account would you probably use to pay bills?

7) Which account would you use to save money?

8) Why do you pay interest on a loan? To whom do you pay it?

More About Credit

A credit reference is a person or bank that will recommend you for a loan or credit. A personal reference is someone who knows you personally. The first time you borrow money or open a charge account, you are establishing credit. When you repay a loan on time, the bank becomes a solid credit reference. If you pay your bills at a department store, the store is also a good credit reference.

Good credit is a history of paying bills and loans on time. Bad credit is a history of late or skipped payments.

A credit limit is the maximum amount that a bank will let you borrow. It can also be the maximum amount a store will allow you to charge.

Credit Application   please print

NAME–FIRST	MIDDLE INITIAL	LAST		AGE (MUST BE AT LEAST 18)
PRESENT ADDRESS–STREET		CITY	STATE	ZIP CODE
TIME AT THIS ADDRESS ____Yrs. ____Mos.	☐ OWN/BUYING ☐ LIVE WITH RELATIVES	☐ RENT ☐ OTHER	DRIVER'S LICENSE NUMBER & STATE	
RESIDENCE TELEPHONE (AREA CODE)		SOCIAL SECURITY NO. (MUST BE PROVIDED)		
IF LESS THAN 3 YEARS AT RESIDENCE, GIVE PREVIOUS ADDRESS			NUMBER OF DEPENDENTS (EXCLUDE APPLICANT)	
EMPLOYED BY			HOW LONG ____Yrs. ____Mos.	BUSINESS PHONE (AREA CODE)
BUSINESS ADDRESS			TYPE OF BUSINESS	
OCCUPATION	YEARLY SALARY	OTHER INCOME*	*Income from alimony, child support or separate maintenance payments need not be revealed if you do not choose to have it considered as a basis for repaying this obligation	
☐ CHECKING ACCOUNT	ACCOUNT NUMBER	FINANCIAL INSTITUTION'S NAME AND ADDRESS		
☐ SAVINGS ACCOUNT	ACCOUNT NUMBER	FINANCIAL INSTITUTION'S NAME AND ADDRESS		
CREDIT CARD	ACCOUNT NUMBER	CREDIT CARD	ACCOUNT NUMBER	
CREDIT REFERENCE	ACCOUNT NUMBER	CREDIT REFERENCE	ACCOUNT NUMBER	

Activity F Write your answers to these questions on your paper.

1) Do you have a bank account? If yes, what type do you have?

2) Do you have any credit references? Name them.

3) Write the name and address of a person who knows you personally and who might help you obtain credit. Do not name a relative or any person who lives in your home.

Establishing Credit

Whenever you try to borrow money, the lender will want to know your credit history. You will probably be asked for credit references. The first time you ask for credit, you do not have a history—good or bad. Here are guidelines for establishing credit:

Step 1   You usually need a regular income before you can establish credit.

Step 2   Open a checking account and a savings account at a bank. Do not overdraw your checking account. Add to your savings account regularly. You can use your bank as a credit reference.

Step 3   Open a charge account at a department store. The store will probably give you a low credit limit. Purchase something with your charge card. When the bill comes each month, pay at least the minimum amount until the item is paid for. Don't buy things unless you need them. Always pay your bill on time. Then your charge account can be a credit reference.

Step 4   Take out a small loan at a bank. Make your payments on time. After you have repaid this loan, you will have another credit reference.

Activity G   Write the answer to these questions on your paper.

1) What is the first thing you could do to establish credit so that you can borrow money to buy a car?

2) What are two kinds of accounts you can open at a bank?

3) What kind of account do you open at a department store?

4) What is a credit limit?

5) What is the most important rule when you take out a loan?

Part A Write on your paper your answers to these questions.

1) What are three kinds of people or businesses that would be good credit references?

2) What kind of person would be a good personal reference?

3) What are three types of bank accounts?

Part B Match the words with their meanings. Write on your paper the correct letter beside each number.

Words

1) Asset
2) Liability
3) Value
4) Loan
5) Interest
6) Credit
7) Finance charge
8) Merchandise
9) Deposit
10) Withdrawal

Meanings

a) Taking money out of a bank account
b) Any property that you own
c) Putting money into an account
d) The amount a buyer will pay
e) A fee for borrowing on credit
f) Money a bank pays on a savings account
g) Goods for sale or that you buy
h) Money you owe; a debt
i) Time that you get to pay for merchandise
j) Money that you have borrowed

Part C Write on your paper a financial statement for Harry Mays. List his assets and liabilities. Compute his net worth.

1) He has a car worth $4,200.00.

2) He has a TV set valued at $300.00

3) He owes $133.81 at Wilton's Department Store.

4) He has a savings account with a balance of $312.80.

5) He has $129.15 in his checking account.

6) He owes the bank $ 2,568.00 on a car loan.

Part A   Each item on this form has a number. Number your paper from 1 to 15. Beside each number, print the information asked for on the form.

---

1. Full name _____

Last   First   Middle   Maiden

2. Present address _____

No. Street or Rural Route City State ZIP

3. Years at this address _____ 4. Phone (____) ____-_____

5. Former address (if less than 2 years at present address)

   _____

No. Street or Rural Route City State ZIP

6. Date of birth __/__/__ 7. Place of birth (city, state) _____

8. U.S. Citizen? Yes ☐ No ☐ 9. If no, name country _____

10. Social Security number _____–_____–_____

11. Father's full name _____

First   Middle   Last

12. Mother's full name at birth _____

First   Middle   Last

13. Your present age ___ 14. Today's date __/__/__

15. Your signature _____

Use the following checklist before going on.

- Did you print your answer neatly?

- Did you answer every question?

- Is the information correct?

- Did you follow the directions exactly?

Part B Write on your paper the word or phrase that completes each sentence. Use the word or phrases in the list. You will not use all of the terms listed.

maiden	finance charge	salary	charge account
position	job application	loan	work experience
interest	credit history	deposit	birth certificate
value	reference	liability	signature
asset	withdrawal	education	

1) A _____ is a form you use to ask for work.
2) A _____ is a person who will recommend you for a job.
3) The money that you earn is called your _____ .
4) Your legal name is on your _____ .
5) Your mother's name at birth is her _____ name.
6) A _____ is the name of a job.
7) Your _____ is all of your school experiences.
8) You write your _____ on a check.
9) An _____ is something that you own.
10) A _____ is a debt that you owe someone.
11) Emilio paid $2,500 for a car. He sold it a year later for $1,900. The _____ of the car was $1,900.
12) Chris put his money into a savings account. Every month the bank paid him _____ .
13) Ruby opened a charge account. When she got her bill, she made a payment. Because she still owed the store money, a _____ was added to her bill.
14) Anne had $100 in her savings account. She made a _____ of $10. Now she has $110 in her account.
15) Mrs. Chang borrowed money from the bank. Now she has a _____ account.

Test Taking Tip When taking a matching test, match all the items that you are certain go together. Cross these items out. Then try to match the items that are left.

Chapter 9

Shopping by Catalog

Many businesses in the United States sell their products through the mail. Instead of selling products to a retail store, they sell them directly to the consumer. Their goods are displayed in a catalog rather than in a store. A catalog is like a reference book. It usually has pictures and descriptions of many kinds of merchandise. People use catalogs for information about products. They also use catalogs for shopping and browsing. When you browse, you read small bits of information at random.

In Chapter 9, you will learn about catalog shopping. Each lesson will help you learn how to read and understand the information in a catalog and how to order merchandise.

Goals for Learning

▶ To learn how to read and understand the information in a catalog

▶ To learn how to order merchandise from a catalog

▶ To learn how to solve problems related to catalog shopping

Advantage
A benefit or positive feature.

Appliance
A piece of household equipment such as a toaster, oven, dishwasher, electric mixer, or microwave oven.

Dealer
A business or individual that sells to the public.

Disadvantage
An unfavorable condition or negative feature.

Retail
Items that are for sale to the public.

Wholesale
The merchandise that is for sale to dealers.

Large department stores and mail order houses have many kinds of merchandise. They buy the merchandise **wholesale** and sell it **retail**. Wholesale refers to the merchandise that is for sale to **dealers**. A dealer is someone who sells to the public. Retail refers to items that are for sale to the public. Dealers sell clothing; **appliances** (a piece of household equipment such as a toaster, oven, dishwasher, electric mixer, or microwave oven); jewelry; furniture; machines and tools; toys and games; and other kinds of goods.

You may buy merchandise from dealers in five ways. You may

- purchase the item in the store.
- order the item by telephone.
- order the item by mail.
- order by computer through an on-line catalog.
- order by FAX.

If you order the item, you may receive it in two ways.

- You may pick up your order at the store.
- The item may be delivered to your home.

Each method of buying merchandise has **advantages** and **disadvantages**. An advantage is a benefit, or a reason, for choosing something. A disadvantage is an unfavorable condition or a reason for not choosing something.

In addition to the price of the goods, customers usually pay mailing costs. Remember to add that cost in when you are comparing prices.

Activity A   Write on your paper one advantage and one disadvantage of buying

1) by phone, computer, or FAX.

2) by mail.

3) at the store.

Catalog Showrooms

Department stores buy goods from manufacturers at **wholesale price**. The wholesale price is the price a manufacturer charges for items bought in large amounts. The **retail price** is what stores charge their customers. The retail price is higher than the wholesale price.

Stores will sometimes offer merchandise at a **sale price**. The sale price is lower than the retail price of a certain item. The sale price is usually for a certain period of time.

In some ways, catalog showrooms are like large department stores and mail order houses.

- They have catalogs that list their merchandise.
- They have stores where you may look at the merchandise.
- They have special sale prices on merchandise.
- You may buy goods at the store.
- You may order through the mail.

Catalog showrooms differ from department stores and mail order houses in some ways.

- Catalog showrooms sell items at a **discount price**. A discount price is below the regular retail price.
- Catalog showrooms usually do not sell as many different items.
- Catalog showrooms have different name brands. Some department stores sell only their own brand.

Activity B   Write on your paper your answers to these questions.

1) Name one way that catalog showrooms are like large department stores.

2) Name one way they are different.

3) Name one advantage of ordering from a large department store catalog.

4) Name one advantage of ordering from a catalog showroom store.

Finding Items in a Catalog

Most large catalogs have an index to help you find quickly what you are looking for. Here is an example of an index with main headings.

Quick Reference Guide

appliances	173–197	jewelry	1–75
automotive	349–356	lamps	232–237
baby goods	386–396	lawn furniture	336–337
billfolds	98–101	luggage	258–266
calculators	270–273	office equipment	274–276
car stereos	355–356	personal care	206–215
clocks	96, 242–253	photographic equipment	280–290
cookware	163–175	radios	291–293
diamonds	1–22	stereo, TVs	294–329
floor care	199–201	sporting goods	347–348
giftware	135–147	tools	338–346
hardware	338–346	toys	397–444

Activity C Read each item below. Then find each item in the index above. Write on your paper the first page of the catalog where the item would be found.

> **EXAMPLE** Jane wants a wallet. A wallet is a billfold. She would look on page 98.

1) Anita is shopping for a vacuum cleaner.
2) Richard needs a suitcase.
3) Kim is looking for some earrings.
4) Gary wants a hammer and a saw.
5) Lorie would like a pretty vase to give to her mother for her birthday.

Comparison Shopping With Catalogs

When you compare prices at different stores, you are doing comparison shopping. You can do comparison shopping with catalogs. When you want to buy a certain item, find it in one or two catalogs. Look at the prices and the different features each product has. Decide which item is the best buy.

Activity D   Use the descriptions of the three kinds of popcorn poppers to answer the questions. Write your answers on your paper.

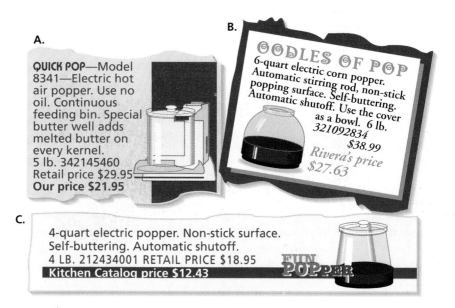

A.

QUICK POP—Model 8341—Electric hot air popper. Use no oil. Continuous feeding bin. Special butter well adds melted butter on every kernel.
5 lb. 342145460
Retail price $29.95
Our price $21.95

B.

OODLES OF POP
6-quart electric corn popper. Automatic stirring rod, non-stick popping surface. Self-buttering. Automatic shutoff. Use the cover as a bowl. 6 lb.
321092834
$38.99
Rivera's price $27.63

C.

4-quart electric popper. Non-stick surface. Self-buttering. Automatic shutoff.
4 LB. 212434001 RETAIL PRICE $18.95
Kitchen Catalog price $12.43
FUN POPPER

1) What does item A use instead of oil?

2) What is the most important difference between items B and C?

3) Which popcorn popper lets you use the cover as a bowl?

4) What is the catalog number of item A?

5) How much money will you save if you buy item A in the catalog rather than at the full retail price?

6) Which popper do you have to unplug to turn off?

7) How much does item C cost through the catalog?

Specialty Catalogs

There are many small mail order catalog businesses. They sell clothing, novelties, gift items, and other sorts of specialty items. Usually there is a picture of each item and a brief description. You must read the descriptions very carefully to be sure of what you are getting.

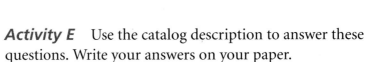

18D. Ripe Tomato Red, striped with cream in soft, supple rayon crepe. Here is a fabulous two-piece dress with a jewel neckline and a softly gathered skirt. Sizes 5-13.
CA4531 $52.00 (4.25—shipping and handling)

Activity E   Use the catalog description to answer these questions. Write your answers on your paper.

1) What is Item 18D—a dress or a matching skirt and blouse?

2) What is the catalog number?

3) What is the price of the item?

4) What sizes of this item can you order?

5) What are the colors of this item?

6) Can you buy it in a different color?

7) What kind of material is this item?

8) What will be the total cost to have the dress delivered to you?

Catalog Descriptions

Catalog descriptions are really advertisements. They use the same type of language used in advertising. The goal of a catalog description is to convince you that your life will be enriched and improved if you buy the product.

Rebate

A return of part of a payment for a product.

Sometimes a catalog description will offer a **rebate**. A rebate is a return of part of the payment for a product or service. Check the description of the product you plan to purchase to see if it includes a rebate or any other special offers.

HOME COMPUTER — Easy to use even if you've never touched a computer before. All you need is some software and your computer is ready to teach, entertain, or help you with home finances at a touch of a button.
Order Model **4432S**.

Our price	$1,624.99
Factory *rebate*	$199.00
Our price	$1,425.99

Monitor and keyboard extra

Activity F Use the catalog description above to answer these questions. Write your answers on your paper.

1) How much money is the store charging the customer for this computer?

2) How much money will the customer get back from the factory after purchasing the computer?

3) What does the ad say the computer can help you do?

4) What is not included in the price of the computer?

5) What is the model number of the computer?

Part A   Write on your paper your answers to these questions.

1) Describe two ways to order merchandise from a catalog.

2) Who pays wholesale prices—customers or dealers?

3) Which kind of price is highest?

     a) wholesale   **b)** retail   **c)** discount

4) What can you use in catalogs to find a certain item quickly?

     a) table of contents   **b)** index   **c)** gazetteer

5) Name one kind of information about goods that you will find in a catalog. (There are several possible answers.)

6) What does it mean when a catalog offers a rebate?

Part B   Read the description. Write on your paper your answers to the questions that follow.

We are happy to introduce more fine porcelain from Brazil in the form of these COFFEE MUGS. The porcelain is thick enough to keep the contents hot, but tapers to a thin rim for easy sipping. The bases are inset for stacking, and the price is designed to please. 8 oz. capac.

Set of four, #123-9902.......................$12.00

1) How many cups will you receive?

2) What is the value of each cup?

3) Are customers offered a choice of colors?

4) In what country were the cups made?

5) What material was used to make these cups?

6) Can you stack these cups?

7) What is the catalog order number?

When you order merchandise by phone or by mail, an extra charge is added because the goods are sent to your home. These charges are called either postage and handling charges or shipping charges. Shipping charges are usually found on the order form. They are computed on the total amount of the order or the weight of the items being shipped.

Shipping Charges by Cost

Amount of order:	Include:
Up to $9.99	$1.95
$10.00 - $19.99	$2.95
$20.00 - $29.99	$3.95
$30.00 - $39.99	$4.95
$40.00 - $49.99	$5.95
$50.00 - $74.99	$7.50
$75.00 - $99.99	$8.25
Over $100.00	$11.00

Shipping Rates by Weight

Lb.	Charge
1 - 5	$3.15
6 - 10	$5.07
11 - 15	$6.98
16 - 20	$8.90
21 - 25	$10.95
26 - 30	$12.78
31 - 40	$16.65
Over 40	$20.54

Activity A   Figure out the total cost of each item in the two ways shown below. Write your answers as in the example.

a) Add shipping charges by cost.

b) Add shipping charges by weight.

> EXAMPLE   Set of 4 10-oz. mugs. Insulated plastic, 2 lb. $3.47.
>
> **a)** $3.47 + $1.95 = $5.42
>
> **b)** $3.47 + $3.15 = $6.62

1) PINE PAPER CUP DISPENSER. Holds about 45 5-oz. cups. 3 lb. Retail price $18.00. Our price $15.00.

2) MAPLE ROCKING CHAIR. Colonial style. 21 lb. $67.97.

3) 10-SPEED BIKE. Big, nobby tires. 26″ chrome frame. 49 lb. $134.95.

4) JOYSTICK REMOTE CONTROLS. 1 lb. Regularly $29.95. Sale price $20.00.

5) EXERCISE BENCH DELUXE MODEL. 67 lb. $109.00.

Ordering by Phone

You may want to order from a catalog store by telephone. When you order by phone, have all the information ready that you will need to place your order. Here is a list of the kind of information usually needed to place a catalog order.

1. Catalog item number

2. Name of item

3. Description (including size and color if applicable)

4. Quantity

5. Price of each item

6. Total price (multiply price of one by the number of items ordered)

7. Shipping weight

8. Credit card number and expiration date

Activity B Choose two items from the list to order by telephone. Make a list of the information you will need about each item to place the order. Write the information on your paper.

A. CAMP STOVE 3 1/2 pt. fuel tank. 22" × 13" × 6". 15 lb. #134200BC **$34.95.**

B. TWO–PERSON TENT Fire retardant–coated nylon with 3-zip screen entrance, rear screen window with storm flap. Polyurethane floor. Rope, poles, stakes. 4 lb. #134210BC **$20.00.**

C. 2 QT. DESERT CANTEEN Blanket covered for insulation. Screw cap with safety chain. Rustproof steel frame. 2 lb. #123200BC **$5.00.**

D. SLEEPING BAG 33" × 75" Ripstop nylon shell, nylon lining. 3 lb. #123400BC **$27.95.**

E. HEAVY DUTY FLASHLIGHT Optically perfect reflector with shatterproof lens. Needs two "D" batteries. 2 lb. #234540DF **$3.05.**

Payment Methods

There are several ways to pay for a catalog order.

Check

A draft on your bank account.

Money order

A check you purchase at the bank or post office for a certain amount of money.

Charge card

An account that allows you to charge the cost of goods to the business that issues the card.

1. **Check**—A check is a draft on your bank account. You mail a check with your order.

2. **Money Order**—You buy a money order from the bank or post office in the amount of your catalog order.

3. **Charge Card**—You may have a charge card for a certain store, or you may use a major credit card. A charge card is an account that allows you to charge the cost of goods to the company that issues the card. When you call to place your order, you give the number of your charge card. Most mail order companies accept major credit cards such as MasterCard and Visa. Large catalog stores offer their own charge accounts.

CUT HERE

Sold To:

Name: _____ Phone: _____

Street Address: _____

City: _____ State: _____ ZIP: _____

PAYMENT METHOD: Do not send cash. Make checks payable to:
Better Products, Inc.

☐ Check or money
   order enclosed
Charge my order to:
☐ MasterCard
☐ VISA   Signature _____
                        Orders not valid without signature.

Credit card number   Exp. Date

Activity C   Use the order form above to answer the following questions. Write your answers on your paper.

1) Does this company accept cash?

2) To what name do you make your check payable?

3) Will the company send your order if you do not write your signature on the form?

4) What two major credit cards may you use to pay for an order?

Filling Out an Order Form

Be sure to fill out order forms very carefully. You want to be sure you get the merchandise you order. If you write the wrong catalog number, you may get the wrong item. If you write your address incorrectly, you may never receive your order.

✂
CUT HERE

Order Form

1. Name _Edward Gomez_
2. Address _9301 Watkins Avenue_
3. City / State / ZIP _Wilton, Delaware   19973_
4. Daytime telephone (_302_) _217-3881_

	Item	#Qty.	Description	Item Price	Total Price
5.	101-0019	1	Wool cap, red	$18.00	$18 00
6.	103-0020	3	Tennis balls, yellow	5.00	15 00

SHIPPING CHARGES
UP TO $10.00 $2.00
$10.00 - $30.00 $3.00
OVER $30.00 $4.00

7. Total Price $ 33 00
8. Shipping   4 00
9. Total Charge $ 37 00

Activity D   Number your paper from 1 to 9 as on the order form above. Choose any two items below to order. Write the information correctly as you would on the order form.

101–0019   WOOL CAPS. One size fits all. Red, blue, green. $18.00.

101–2001   WARM-UP SUIT. 100% polyester. S-M-L-XL. Blue or green. $59.95.

102–1001   BASEBALL GLOVE in fine quality leather. $49.95.

103–0020   TENNIS BALLS. Yellow or orange. Special sale price. $5.00.

104–1008   VIDEOCASSETTE RECORDER, VHS format. $195.00.

Part A Write on your paper your answers to these questions.

1) Name two ways to order from a catalog.

2) Who is responsible for paying shipping charges—the catalog dealer or the customer?

3) What are two ways to pay for a catalog order?

4) Give an example of a major credit card.

✂ CUT HERE

Order Form

1. Name _____

2. Address _____

3. City / State / ZIP _____

4. Daytime telephone (———)——————————

	Item	#Qty.	Description	Item Price	Total Price
5.					
6.					

SHIPPING CHARGES	
UP TO $10.00	$2.00
$10.00 - $30.00	$3.00
OVER $30.00	$4.00

7. Total Price $

8. Shipping

9. Total Charge $

Part B Number your paper from 1 to 9 as on the order form. Choose any two items below to order. Write the information as you would on the order form on your paper.

702222 RUBY PENDANT. 3 rubies and 2 diamonds in 10K gold $335.00.

34311W ELEGANT WATCH. 6-digit, displays hours, minutes, seconds, months, and days on command . . . Sale-priced $84.95.

21333A BRASS COAT TREE. Traditional hall stand in polished brass. 6′ high. $89.90 or two for $165.00.

Sometimes the merchandise you order will be unsatisfactory in some way.

EXAMPLES	You may receive broken items.
	The item may not work properly.
	Clothing may not fit.
	Merchandise may not look like the picture in the catalog.
	You may not like the merchandise.

It is important to examine the merchandise carefully as soon as it arrives. You have two choices. You can

1. wrap the item up and mail it back. Explain what is wrong in a letter.

2. take it back to the store. Tell the manager what is wrong.

Whatever your choice, you should return the merchandise as quickly as possible.

What the Store Will Do

How a store responds when you return an item is partly your choice. Some stores will not return your money, especially if the item is on sale. However, a store may

1. give you another item that fits or isn't broken.

2. fix the item if it is broken.

3. return the full amount of your purchase price in cash.

4. apply a credit to your credit card if you purchased the item this way.

5. give you a store credit to use to buy something else.

A Letter of Complaint

Here is a letter that Chris Williams wrote when she returned a dress.

31 E. Ralston Pl.
Wilton, DE 19999

April 3, 1999

Dress AMERICA
P.O. Box 231
Selbyville, TX 75820

Attention: Customer Service

Dear Sir:
   I am returning the dress #CA4531 Size 11.
It is too large. Please exchange it for a size 9.
Thank you for your help.

Sincerely,

Chris Williams

Chris Williams

Activity A   Write a letter of complaint to the following address. Use the letter above as an example. Address the letter to

Quality Products, Inc.
12 West Franklin Street
Wilkinsburg, PA 15220
Attention: Customer Service

Choose one of these problems to write about:

1) Your videotape recorder isn't working properly. It will not eject the tape.

2) A set of dishes you planned to give your sister for her new apartment arrived broken.

3) Your popcorn maker is not shutting off automatically. The popcorn is burning.

When More Action Is Needed

Your other attempts to clear up an unsatisfactory order may not work. If that happens, here are some more steps to take when action is needed.

1. If a catalog store does not take action on your complaint within a few weeks, call them on the telephone. Use the toll-free number or call collect. Ask to speak with a manager or supervisor.

2. Contact the post office if your order was sent through the mail. Give them all the information they need to trace your letter or package. They will need to know the name of the company, the complete mailing address, the telephone number with area code, the date it was mailed, and how it was mailed.

3. Many newspapers and television stations have people who investigate consumer problems. Find out their address and write to them for help.

4. Write the store another letter. Be persistent! Don't give up until the problem is solved.

5. Contact the Better Business Bureau. Find out how they rate the company. File a complaint with them if necessary.

6. Review all of your letters and any notes from phone calls. See if you overlooked anything that would clear up the matter or would help you take more action.

Lesson Review   Number your paper from 1 to 4. Read each problem below and choose the best solution. Write the correct letter beside each number.

Problems

1) Charles ordered a shirt from the World's Horizon catalog. When the shirt came, it was the wrong size.

2) Sandy bought a set of dishes at a catalog showroom. When she got home and opened the box, she found a broken plate.

3) Lily Collins ordered a blouse from a catalog through the mail. The blouse did not look like the one in the picture. Lily wants her money back.

4) Justin returned his computer to Quality Products, Inc. In a few weeks, they sent it back. It still did not work.

Solutions

a) Mail the merchandise back immediately. Explain what is wrong. Tell the store the size you need.

b) Mail the merchandise back at once. Tell the store you want your money refunded.

c) Call the company. Explain the problem.

d) Take the merchandise back to the store as soon as possible.

Chapter 9 Review

Part A Number your paper from 1 to 10. Match the terms with their meanings. Write the correct letter next to each number.

Terms

1) Catalog
2) Merchandise
3) Reference book
4) Advantage
5) Disadvantage
6) Compare
7) Retail price
8) Check
9) Major credit card
10) Money order

Meanings

a) VISA or MasterCard
b) A book with information
c) To decide how things are different or alike
d) Cost of an item in a store
e) A draft on your bank account
f) Any item for sale
g) A reason to choose something
h) A reason not to choose something
i) A purchased document that is used to pay someone
j) Any list of items

Part B Write on your paper the word that completes each sentence. Use one of the words from the box.

discount	sale
retail	wholesale

1) Jack paid the suggested _____ price for his new coat.

2) The coat that Anna bought was on _____.

3) The catalog store sold merchandise at a _____ price.

4) The dealer paid the _____ price for her merchandise.

Part C   Read the product description below. On your paper, write the information as you would on the order form shown.

#054-9856

Telephone Answering Machine

Call from anywhere in the world and pick up messages. Built-in speaker and earphone jack.

Sale-priced at $125.95

✂ CUT HERE

Order Form

1. Name _____

2. Address _____

3. City / State / ZIP _____

4. Daytime telephone (___) _____

	Item	#Qty.	Description	Item Price	Total Price
5.					
6.					

SHIPPING CHARGES	
UP TO $10.00	$2.00
$10.00 - $30.00	$3.00
OVER $30.00	$4.00

7. Total Price $
8. Shipping
9. Total Charge $

Part D   Explain what you would do to solve the problem described below. Write your answer on your paper.

> You ordered a light blue sweatshirt from a catalog to give to your brother for his birthday. You checked with the operator to be sure that you would receive the sweatshirt in time. However, it arrived late. On top of that, the sweatshirt was the wrong size *and* the wrong color.

Test Taking Tip   When studying for a test, memorize only the most important points. Practice writing or saying the material out loud. Have a partner listen to check if you are right.

Glossary

A

Abbreviation—a shortened form of a written word (p. 29)

Accent mark—a mark that shows which part of a word to stress when pronouncing the word (p. 28)

Advantage—a benefit or positive feature (p. 248)

Advertise—to announce something to the public through the media (p. 192)

Advertisement—a public notice, usually about a product or service for sale (p. 189)

Affiliate—a member station that carries some of the programs broadcast by a large television network (p. 210)

Alphabetical order—the order of letters of the alphabet (p. 2)

Alternative—a choice between two or more possibilities (p. 109)

Antonym—a word that means the opposite of another word (p. 50)

Appliance—a piece of household equipment such as a toaster, oven, dishwasher, electric mixer, or microwave oven (p. 248)

Applicable—something that is appropriate or suitable (p. 227)

Application—a form to make a request (p. 226)

Apprentice—a worker being trained by an experienced and skilled person (p. 167)

Assets—property you own that has value (p. 237)

Associate's degree—a degree from a two-year college or a community college (p. 158)

Atlas—a book of maps and geographical facts (p. 63)

Autobiography—a story of a real person's life written by that person (p. 132)

Available—refers to when you can begin a job (p. 226)

B

Bachelor's degree—a degree from a four-year college or university (p. 158)

Back issue—an issue that was published in the past (p. 148)

Benefits—what workers receive in addition to wages, such as health insurance and vacations (p. 202)

Bibliography—a list of books and articles an author has used as references to write a book; bibliographies usually appear in the back of the book (p. 137)

Biographical dictionary—a reference book that lists famous people and facts about their lives (p. 50)

Biographical novel—a fictional account of a real person's life (p. 132)

Biography—a nonfiction book about a real person written by someone other than that person (p. 132)

Blue pages—a part of the telephone book that lists the numbers of government agencies (p. 120)

Branch—one of the libraries in a system of libraries (p. 128)

Broadcast—to send radio or television signals through the air to receivers in the home, the car, or other location (p. 206)

Bureau—a specialized group or department that focuses on one area or one main topic (p. 171)

C

Call number—the numbers and letters assigned to a library book; the call number determines where the book will be placed on the shelf (p. 137)

Cartoon—usually a single drawing that the artist uses to tell a joke or express an idea (p. 183)

Catalog—any list of information (p. 129)

CD-ROM—a computer science term that stands for *compact disc read-only memory* (p. 58)

Chapter—a part of a book (p. 18)

Charge card—an account that allows you to charge the cost of goods to the business that issues the card (p. 257)

Check—a draft on your bank account (p. 257)

Circulate—can be taken out of the library (p. 147)

Classified advertisements—short public notices (items for sale, apartments or houses for rent, help wanted) (p. 181)

Column—a regular newspaper feature about recent events, current political and social issues, and other topics of interest to readers (p. 181)

Columnist—a person who writes from a personal point of view on events and issues and on how problems can be solved (p. 182)

Comic strip—a series of cartoon frames that tell a story (p. 183)

Condensed—a shorter version of an article but with the same main idea (p. 92)

Consumer—someone who buys and uses goods and services (p. 173)

Consumers Union—a group that tests products and investigates businesses; the Consumers Union publishes the results of its tests in a magazine called *Consumer Reports* (p. 173)

Contractor—a person who agrees to perform work or to provide supplies for a job (p. 167)

Credentials—proof that a person is an expert in a certain area of work (p. 158)

Credit—the time you get to pay for the goods you buy (p. 239)

Cross reference—a related topic you can look up to find additional information on a topic; a cross reference directs you to another part or section of the book (p. 20)

Current—up to the present (p. 180)

Current issue—the most recently published issue of a magazine (p. 148)

Cycle—the period of time between events, such as the publishing of a magazine (p. 93)

D

Daily—every day (p. 180)

Dealer—a business or individual that sells to the public (p. 248)

Death notice—information about a person's death and details about the funeral arrangements (p. 183)

Debt—money owed, or liability (p. 237)

Deposit—the money you put into an account (p. 240)

Derived—to come from (p. 37)

Dewey Decimal System—a system that libraries use to classify and organize books (p. 137)

Dialogue—conversation (p. 132)

Dictionary—a book that contains an alphabetical listing of words and their meanings (p. 26)

Digest—a magazine that contains summaries or condensed articles from other magazines (p. 92)

Disadvantage—an unfavorable condition or negative feature (p. 248)

Discount price—a price below the regular retail price (p. 249)

Doctoral degree—the highest degree awarded by a university or professional school (p. 159)

Document—a paper that gives information to another person (p. 220)

Documentary—a nonfiction film or television program (p. 214)

Donation—a gift of money or other items of value (p. 210)

E

Edit—to get written material ready for publication (p. 145)

Editor—a person who decides which stories will be reported to the public (p. 187)

Editorial—opinion about an issue or event in the news; editorials are written by members of the newspaper staff (p. 182)

Education—a combination of the courses and programs taken at a school or college (p. 228)

Employee—a person who works for someone else (p. 226)

Employer—a person or company that pays you a salary (p. 226)

Encyclopedia—a book or set of books with a collection of articles and facts on many subjects, organized in alphabetical order (p. 71)

Entry—a listing in a dictionary; an entry provides facts about a word (p. 26)

Equator—an imaginary line that circles the center of the earth (p. 69)

Etymology—the study of the history of a word (p. 37)

Executive—a manager, a supervisor, or an administrator (p. 202)

Experience—the same kind of work that you have done before (p. 202)

Expert—a person with training and knowledge about a specific subject (p. 158)

F

Farmer's almanac—an annual calendar of days, weeks, and months with weather predictions and astronomical facts (p. 58)

Federal Communications Commission (FCC)—a government agency that provides licenses to people or companies to operate television and radio stations (p. 214)

Fee—a charge for a service (p. 102)

Fiction—an imaginary story (p. 132)

Finance charge—a fee you pay on money you owe to a business (p. 239)

Financial—concerning money or property with value (p. 237)

Foreman—a supervisor or boss (p. 167)

Form—a printed or typed document with spaces to fill in information (p. 220)

Former—refers to something that happened in the past (p. 226)

Full name—a person's whole legal name (p. 220)

Full time—a job that requires approximately 40 hours per week, or 8 hours a day for 5 days (p. 202)

G

Gazetteer—a dictionary of geographical place names (p. 63)

General information almanac—an almanac that contains facts and figures about a variety of subjects from the previous year and from the past (p. 59)

Geographical dictionary—a reference book with a list of rivers, mountains, cities, and other features (p. 50)

Gimmick—an important feature about something that is kept secret (p. 190)

Globe—a model of the earth; it shows the actual placement of the continents, islands, and oceans (p. 65)

Grid—a network of lines on a map that makes it possible to locate specific places (p. 66)

Grid map—a map with grid lines (p. 66)

Guide words—words at the top of a page of information given in alphabetical order; all words that come in alphabetical order between the two guide words can be found on that page (p. 6)

H

Historical novel—a fictional story about real people and events (p. 132)

History—a nonfiction book about real people and events of the past (p. 132)

Homonym—a word that sounds exactly like another word but is spelled differently and has a different meaning (p. 45)

Horizontal—a word that means going across (p. 66)

How-to books—reference books that provide detailed instructions for how to complete specific tasks (p. 87)

I

Independent contractors—people in business for themselves (p. 167)

Index—an alphabetical list of main topics covered in a book (p. 18)

Interest—the money a bank pays you for putting money into a savings account; the fee you pay for borrowing money (p. 240)

Internet—the largest computer network in the world; it allows people from all over the world to use computers to interact with one another and to get information on a wide variety of topics (p. 87)

Interval—the space of time between events (p. 91)

Itemized—listed one by one (p. 110)

J

Joint—an account that is shared or owned together (p. 239)

Journeyman—a worker who has completed an apprenticeship and passed a test (p. 167)

K

Key—a guide to symbols and abbreviations (p. 26)

Key word—a word that names what you want to find out about (p. 13)

L

Latitude lines—the horizontal lines on a map that indicate east to west (p. 68)

Lead—the first paragraph of a news story; summarizes the most important facts in the story and answers the questions *Who? What? Where?* and *When?* (p. 187)

Liability—the money you owe (p. 237)

Library catalog—a catalog that lists most of the materials in a library; there are three types of listings: title, author, and subject (p. 129)

Library of Congress—the national library of the United States (p. 130)

Loan—a sum of money that you borrow (p. 238)

Local—having to do with one certain place (p. 180)

Longitude lines—the vertical lines on a map that indicate north to south (p. 68)

M

Magazine—a paperback publication with stories and articles on a variety of topics by different writers (p. 91)

Magazine catalog—a catalog that lists all the magazines a library subscribes to and identifies the issues the library has (p. 129)

Maiden name—a woman's last name before she marries (p. 220)

Mass media—a way to communicate with the most people at one time; for example: television, radio, newspapers, and magazines (p. 180)

Master's degree—an advanced degree, beyond a bachelor's degree, from a graduate school or university (p. 159)

Master's level—a worker who has more experience than a journeyman and has passed another test; this worker has earned a master's license (p. 167)

Merchandise—goods for sale or that you buy (p. 239)

Microfiche—a film card on which many pages of reduced copy are stored (p. 129)

Money order—a check you purchase at the bank or post office for a certain amount of money (p. 257)

N

National—having to do with a whole country, or nation (p. 180)

Net worth—the value of your assets minus the value of your liabilities (p. 237)

Nonfiction—based on facts (p. 132)

Novel—a long, complex story (p. 132)

O

Obituary—a short article about someone who has recently died (p. 183)

Occupation—the regular work or business a person does (p. 158)

Organization—a group of people united for a common cause (p. 171)

Origin—the beginning of something (p. 37)

P

Part time—a job that requires less than 40 hours per week (p. 202)

Periodical—a magazine published at regular intervals, such as daily, weekly, or monthly (p. 91)

Permanent—a job that is expected to last a long time (p. 202)

Personal information—facts about yourself (p. 220)

Pertinent—applicable (p. 229)

Physical map—a map that shows the roughness of the earth's surface (p. 65)

Political map—a map that shows the boundaries of states and countries (p. 65)

Position—the name of your job (p. 226)

Predominance—being most frequent or common (p. 84)

Preface—an introduction to a book (p. 18)

Previous—refers to something that happened in the past (p. 226)

Prime time—the hours when television is watched the most, between 8 P.M. and 11 P.M. (p. 208)

Product map—a map that has symbols that show where goods are grown or produced (p. 65)

Products—goods that you can buy (p. 112)

Profession—a job that requires special information and training (p. 116)

Professional—someone who works at a specific profession (p. 116)

Publish—to print and distribute magazines, books, newspapers, or other reading materials (p. 93)

Q

Qualifications—a description of your skills and work experience (p. 202)

R

The Readers' Guide to Periodical Literature—a magazine found in the library that lists articles from many other magazines (p. 96)

Rebate—a return of part of a payment for a product (p. 252)

Recipe—a list of ingredients and directions for the preparation of a specific food (p. 77)

Reference book—a book that contains facts about a specific topic or on several topics (p. 18)

References—people who know about your work and who will recommend you for a job (p. 202)

Related topic—a topic connected in some way to another topic (p. 16)

Reliable—a worker who is dependable and does what he or she is expected to do (p. 202)

Reporter—a person who researches facts and writes stories for a newspaper (p. 187)

Resident—a person who lives in a certain place (p. 102)

Retail—items that are for sale to the public (p. 248)

Retail price—the price a customer pays for an item (p. 249)

Road map—a map that shows roads, highways, towns, and other useful travel information (p. 65)

S

Salary—the amount of money you are paid for working (p. 226)

Sale price—a lower price on a certain item for a certain time period (p. 249)

Scale—the relationship shown between distances on the map and actual distances (p. 63)

Service—what a business or individual can do for you (p. 112)

Short story—a story that can usually be read in one sitting (p. 132)

Signature—the name of a person written by that person (p. 220)

Slogan—a word or phrase that is repeated over and over again that expresses the main idea of a product, business, political group, or other organization (p. 190)

Stress—to pronounce a syllable with more emphasis than the other syllables in the word (p. 28)

Subscriber—a customer of a local cable television company (p. 210)

Subscription—a regular order for a magazine, newspaper, or other publication (p. 94)

Subtopic—a topic that is part of a larger topic (p. 13)

Supervisor—a person who is your boss (p. 226)

Syllable—a part of a word with one vowel sound (p. 28)

Symbol—a sign or mark that stands for something else (p. 63)

Synonym—a word with the same or nearly the same meaning as another word (p. 14)

T

Table of contents—a list of the chapters or sections of a book and the page numbers on which the chapters or sections begin (p. 18)

Temporary—a job that lasts for a limited amount of time (p. 202)

Toll-free—a long-distance number with an 800 area code (p. 107)

Topic (subject)—what you want to find out about (p. 13)

Trade—an occupation that requires manual or mechanical skill (p. 167)

V

Value—the amount of money your property is worth to a buyer (p. 237)

Vertical—a word that means going up and down (p. 66)

Vertical file—a file that contains pamphlets and other materials too small to put on a shelf (p. 152)

Video catalog—a catalog that lists films or videotapes that a library owns by title or subject (p. 129)

Volume—a single book, or one book in a set of books (p. 71)

W

White pages—a part of the telephone book with residential, business, and government listings arranged in alphabetical order (p. 102)

Wholesale—the merchandise that is for sale to dealers (p. 248)

Wholesale price—the price a manufacturer charges a dealer for items bought in large amounts (p. 249)

Withdrawal—money that you have taken out of your bank account (p. 240)

Y

Yellow pages—a part of the telephone book with business listings that are organized under subject headings arranged in alphabetical order (p. 104)

Index